# Why Do You Need This New Edition?

If you're wondering why you should buy this new edition of *Steps for Writers: Sentences and Paragraphs to the Essay Volume 1, Second Edition*, here are eight good reasons.

1. New "Stepping Up" tips at the beginning of every chapter introduce you to the main topic area that the chapter will cover and give you a "heads-up" on what you should master by the end of the course.

2. A new section on "Key Words" has been added to the end of each chapter. This brief feature will help you to develop your vocabulary and prepare you for future coursework.

3. New material on outlining has been added to Chapter 1.

4. A whole new section in Chapter 10 on Writing under Pressure: Facing Exams provides advice on how to do your best on timed writing tests.

5. New explanations have been added in Chapter 11 clarifying the differences among revising, editing, and proofreading your work.

6. A sample paragraph with proofreader's corrections has been added in Chapter 11.

7. Many new exercises and sample paragraphs have updated content that reflects current events and social and cultural developments.

8. The quick reference guide to topics on grammar helps you find appropriate grammar topic areas quickly.

Use *Steps for Writers* alongside Pearson's **MyWritingLab** (www.mywritinglab.com) and master content like never before while simultaneously accessing the other MyWritingLab elements that will im results!

D1115465

**PEARSON**

# PRAISE FOR
# STEPS FOR WRITERS

## Sentences and Paragraphs to the Essay, 2e

### VOLUME 1

"I think that my students would find the style appealing and at their reading level . . . The writing is stylistically consistent."

—Debra Favre,
*Mt. San Antonio College*

"The Eggers text is clearly written and designed. The student doesn't become overwhelmed by too many boxes, shaded areas, and bullet points. It is easy to follow the instruction, and the examples of correct and incorrect grammar are thoughtfully chosen."

—Sara Mortimer-Boyd,
*Los Angeles Pierce College*

"We chose Eggers because it covered all aspects of our course's curriculum. The organization fits with our course quite well. Steps for Writers, Volume I is effective—it follows the same layout as textbook on writing essays, but focuses at the paragraph level and I think this is appropriate and useful. I prefer a text which lays out the information, provides examples, and asks students to apply what they have learned—this text does just that."

—Sarah Dangelantonio,
*Franklin Pierce University*

"The conceptualization is strong; examples are numerous, and explanations are clear. My students felt they had learned a great deal from working with Steps for Writers, Volume I."

—Jan Strever,
*Spokane Community College*

"The samples are ideal as they mimic and represent similar writing the students would be expected to write. Other books present samples that are much longer than the students would be asked to produce. Most of the paragraph samples are on target as what the students should aim for in the variety of lengths for college writing. The style and presentation of the material was impressive."

—Alette Corley,
*Bethune Cookman University*

"The three major strengths are conciseness, style (avoiding cumbersome, overly grammatical explanations), and cost."

—Kelly Ormsby,
*Cleveland State Community College*

# about the author

A native of Indiana, PHILIP EGGERS received his A.B., M.A., and Ph.D. in English from Columbia University. He was professor and chairperson of the English Department at Borough of Manhattan Community College of the City University of New York, where for many years he has taught developmental writing and composition, as well as English, American, and world literature. As department chair, he helped create the Writing and Literature Program at BMCC, which is nourishing much undergraduate writing talent. Professor Eggers was elected co-chair of the CUNY English Discipline Council and participated in a CUNY Mellon Seminar and two NEH Summer Seminars. He has presented and moderated at such forums as the CUNY CAWS (City University Association of Writing Supervisors) conferences and NEMLA (Northeast Modern Language Association). He is also a member of Phi Beta Kappa. In addition to a book on Tennyson and articles in scholarly journals on English and American literature, he has written textbooks, including *Writing Skillful Sentences* and *Process and Practice*. Currently Professor Eggers is teaching as emeritus professor, writing, and presenting talks on literature and composition. He continues to enjoy being a father and grandfather, jogging, exploring global literature, and finding time to travel.

PENGUIN ACADEMICS

# STEPS FOR WRITERS
## SENTENCES AND PARAGRAPHS
## TO THE ESSAY

**SECOND EDITION**
**VOLUME 1**

## Philip Eggers

Borough of Manhattan Community College
The City University of New York

**Pearson**

Boston   Columbus   Indianapolis   New York   San Francisco   Upper Saddle River
Amsterdam   Cape Town   Dubai   London   Madrid   Milan   Munich   Paris   Montreal   Toronto
Delhi   Mexico City   Sao Paulo   Sydney   Hong Kong   Seoul   Singapore   Taipei   Tokyo

Senior Acquisitions Editor: Matthew Wright
Marketing Manager: Kurt Massey
Senior Supplements Editor: Donna Campion
Production Manager: Jennifer Bossert
Project Coordination, Text Design, and Electronic Page Makeup: S4Carlisle Publishing Services
Cover Design Manager: Wendy Ann Fredericks
Cover Photo: © Anderson Ross/Blend Images/Age Fotostock
Senior Manufacturing Buyer: Roy Pickering
Printer and Binder: Edwards Brothers
Cover Printer: Lehigh-Phoenix Color/ Hagerstown

For more information about the Penguin Academics series, please contact us by mail at Pearson Education, attn. Marketing Department, 51 Madison Avenue, 28 th Floor, New York, NY 10010, or visit us online at www.pearsonhighered.com/english.

Credits and acknowledgments borrowed from other sources and reproduced, with permission, in this textbook appear on the appropriate page within text [or on page 209].

Library of Congress Cataloging-in-Publication Data
Eggers, Philip.
  Steps for writers : sentences and paragraphs to the essay, volume 1 / Philip Eggers.
    p. cm. — (Penguin Academics)
  Includes bibliographical references and index.
  ISBN-13: 978-0-205-11043-8 (alk. paper)
  ISBN-10: 0-205-11043-6 (alk. paper)
  1.  English language—Rhetoric.  2.  English language—Grammar—Problems, exercises, etc.  3.  Report writing—Problems, exercises, etc.  I. Title.
  PE1408.E3595 2013
  808'.042—dc23
                                                                    2011028489

Copyright © 2013, 2008 by Pearson Education, Inc.

All rights reserved. Manufactured in the United States of America. This publication is protected by Copyright, and permission should be obtained from the publisher prior to any prohibited reproduction, storage in a retrieval system, or transmission in any form or by any means, electronic, mechanical, photocopying, recording, or likewise. To obtain permission(s) to use material from this work, please submit a written request to Pearson Education, Inc., Permissions Department, One Lake Street, Upper Saddle River, New Jersey 07458, or you may fax your request to 201-236-3290.

1 2 3 4 5 6 7 8 9 10—EDW—16 15 14 13 12

www.pearsonhighered.com

ISBN-10: 0-205-11043-6
ISBN-13: 978-0-205-11043-8

# contents

# to the Instructor

Basic writing instruction has come a long way since the 1960s and 1970s, when U.S. colleges, especially the newly created community colleges, opened their doors to a new population of students. English professors of previous generations had assumed, although not always justifiably, that once students entered college, they had already mastered basic skills. The writing instructor's job was to certify, through grades and comments of approval or disapproval, the college-level performance of undergraduate writers. Teaching basic skills, such as punctuation, the correct use of word forms, sentence mastery, and paragraph construction, was regarded as belonging almost entirely to the pre-college curriculum. Changes in higher education, however, redefined the writing instructor's role to include instruction in basics that presumably were taught at a lower level, but often were not—or at least were often not learned and retained. In addition, a large percentage of students in U.S. colleges today are not native speakers of English. They range from those who began learning English in childhood after speaking another language at home to those who only recently arrived in the United States and are just beginning their acquisition of a second language.

Several generations of college students and teachers have faced the challenges brought by these changes. Writing instruction has survived the strains placed on it by the new demands and has changed accordingly. Consequently, few of today's young instructors experience culture shock when they read college essays badly marred by grammatical errors, garbled syntax, and confused organization. And most of us senior faculty willingly continue to accept the challenge of basic writing instruction because we know that our public school systems, which were not originally designed to prepare all students for college work and are therefore inadequately funded to perform that task, cannot meet all the needs of underprepared students. Attempting to compensate for inadequate schooling, second language problems, and cultural forces working against academic achievement in our society continues to be a daunting but inspirational undertaking.

With the advent of communications technology and the pervasiveness of the commercial media throughout every corner of our lives, not to mention the advent of social networking, we confront new challenges and a new set of opportunities when we teach students to write. Ours has become an exciting and frustrating age in which to teach college writing. Inspired by the examples of popular novels being made into blockbuster films, by the Harry Potter books setting astonishing sales records, and by celebrities of all sorts publishing best-selling memoirs, more students than ever hope to become novelists, poets, and journalists. However, a small and shrinking percentage of students arrive at college with a mastery of basic skills and a rich vocabulary. The disparity between aspirations and aptitude has never been wider.

As a result, our mentoring tasks have altered somewhat. In the past, writing instructors—knowing that many students feared writing and were aware of their deficiencies—often felt the need to reassure students and to help them build confidence and overcome anxieties. For some students, of course, that will always remain the chief problem. Today's undergraduates, however, have grown up texting one another and witnessing books written by unskilled authors becoming bestsellers. A new problem, then, added to the lack of confidence afflicting some students is the overconfidence of others. Many do not believe they need writing instruction, either because they think they already know how to write or because they expect someone else to edit and proofread their work.

The graduated approach of *Steps for Writers* is designed to cope with both problems. Students whose confidence needs to be bolstered can begin with basic exercises and assignments that are easy enough to manage. They will be able to experience success before confronting more difficult tasks. Students who are impatient and overconfident will face the reality check of exercises and assignments that will challenge their overconfidence while allowing them to move forward quickly in areas where they are genuinely proficient.

The graduated approach addresses another problem that we face in teaching basic skills: the need to reinforce students' mastery of fundamentals as they become more sophisticated, informed, and literate. We often shake our heads at the recurrence of basic errors in the writing of upper-level undergraduates and even graduate students. We sometimes forget that many features of language, such as subject–verb agreement and agreement of pronouns and antecedents, become considerably more difficult to execute correctly in the complicated sentences appropriate to advanced intellectual work. It should be no wonder, then, that at the end of a basic writing course, students whose vocabulary and mastery of complex sentence structure has advanced measurably may seem to have lost their grip on the grammatical rules they supposedly learned in the course. We have to remember that progress in writing occurs gradually, concurrent with general education, and follows an uneven path, with setbacks in one area, rapid advancement in another, and overall improvement that can only be measured accurately over periods of time longer than a college semester.

Volume 1 of *Steps for Writers* helps students coordinate their skills across the compositional spectrum from word- and sentence-level proficiency through paragraph construction to the planning of essays. The primary focus is on the paragraph as a compositional unit, whereas in Volume 2 the emphasis is on the whole essay. At all times, however, the student is reminded of the need to attain fluency through prolific informal writing and of the need to develop his or her own successful writing process. Students are encouraged to work on fluency and correctness simultaneously, as both are important and neither should be delayed until the other is achieved.

Because every student writer is different, texts and instructors have to be flexible. You may choose to follow the sequence of chapters in *Steps for Writers* as the basis for a syllabus, but many instructors prefer not to structure their course on the table of contents of any text. Although you will probably want to follow the general progression of the three major steps, the sequence of chapters within each step need not be taken as strictly chronological. The experience of learning to write has often been described as recursive, and any book or course should recognize the cycles and repetitions inherent in the process, while at the same time always emphasizing the large goal of growth and development. The definition of one mode as more advanced than another has to be somewhat arbitrary, as narrative can be highly complex and argumentation can be simple. Nevertheless, it is usually easier for students to write experiential essays before engaging in textual analysis or research writing.

*Steps for Writers* is based on the assumption that we are teaching writing as a means of learning, perhaps as the most important activity in students' intellectual maturation. The importance of writing in recent years has been underscored by state legislatures enacting laws requiring writing in public colleges, by university systems mandating proficiency tests, and by the SAT and other tests incorporating writing assessment in the measures used for college admissions. Writing Across the Curriculum and Writing in the Disciplines have become standard practice in nearly every university. There has been a concomitant emphasis on critical thinking in composition pedagogy, no doubt because we perceive that students are vulnerable to the worst kinds of bias and manipulation, from the blandishments of advertising and the specious claims of political leaders to the urban legends found on Web sites. Along with the emphasis on critical thinking, has come a welcome emphasis on creative thinking, not just in courses labeled Creative Writing, but in academic and career writing as well. Being able to propose solutions to problems, formulate original thesis statements, and employ vivid, resourceful diction and style requires creative thinking analogous to the inventiveness displayed by poets and novelists. Fiction and poetry in turn also involve critical thinking. Resisting the tendency to bifurcate critical and creative writing, *Steps for Writers* encourages students to take an interest in both aspects of their writing and incorporates some fiction and poetry among other kinds of professional writing as prose models. Students are likely to feel empowered and to enjoy their writing more if their logical and imaginative faculties are brought into play conjointly.

The Instructor's Manual that accompanies *Steps for Writers* includes an introduction covering, among other subjects, a discussion of the unique challenges of teaching in the 21st century, along with appropriate instructor/student expectations, and coordinating class work with homework. Next are sections to aid instructors in teaching paragraph writing and revising, followed by information on expanding to the essay. The author includes references to books, articles, and journals appropriate to the course, concluding with answers to the exercises in the text.

# Preface to the Second Edition

Students and teachers who have used the first edition of *Steps for Writers* have been enthusiastic about the major features of the book. They like its graduated "steps" arrangement, its compact format, its direct style, and its models of student and professional writing. No text, however, is perfect, and the experience of students and professors is always useful in revealing ways a successful text can be made still better. Furthermore, in a rapidly changing world, textbooks need to keep pace with new directions in teaching, learning, technology, culture, and society.

In this new edition, a number of changes have been made in the organization and format to enhance the effectiveness of *Steps for Writers*. In addition, new material has been added or inserted to replace originals to keep students' learning close to the world they are experiencing, with all its rapid transformations—its popular culture, world events, politics, sports, business, and news.

### New Features of the Second Edition

- New Stepping Up tips at the beginning of each chapter
- A section on outlining in Chapter 1
- A paragraph of proofread text in Chapter 11
- A new section in Chapter 10 on Writing under Pressure: Facing Exams
- Updated content in exercises to reflect current events and social and cultural developments
- Key words at the end of each chapter for review
- A Quick Reference guide to topics of grammar

## Acknowledgments

I am deeply grateful to the following professors who, by their comments, have made this a better textbook: Kathryn Vincent, Washtenaw Community College; Anetia Ports, St. Philip's College; Matt Mathesius, Columbia Basin College; Linda Matthews, South Suburban College; Carolee Ritter, Southeast Community College; and Trisha Dandurand, Kanakakee Community College.

I am indebted as well to the editors who have contribution to the project, first, to Matthew Wright, who guided this book through its original planning and I also wish to thank Jean Smith, developmental production editor of S4Carlisle Publishing Services, for providing expert editorial guidance in the revision of this volume and to Cyndy Taylor, who oversaw the Instuctor's Manual. Finally, I owe much to my colleagues and students at the Borough of Manhattan Community College, from whom I have learned most of what I know about teaching and whose advice and examples have taught me so much about all aspects of writing. Among these colleagues, I especially want to thank Maria do Carmo de Vasconcelos, Joyce Harte, Frank Elmi, Bob Lapides, Nancy McClure, Elliot Podwill, Anthony Drago, Milton Baxter, and Steve Cogan for many years of stimulating exchanges on teaching, writing, and literature.

# to the student

## How to Use This Book

**You will learn to write by doing lots of writing, all kinds of writing**. In this book you will work with paragraphs and the words and sentences on which they are built. This practice will help you to compose, revise, and correct your work more effectively and to move on to the task of composing whole essays. Even at the beginning, however, you should not limit yourself to writing isolated paragraphs or sentences, as valuable as that practice is. Do some informal writing on your own every day. Your command of correct English should grow along with your ability to write fluently, to get thoughts down on the page. If you make it a habit to write frequently, the graduated exercises in this book will help you master basic writing skills, understand how grammatical patterns work, and develop confidence. You will concentrate on learning how to use words and sentences correctly and effectively and to craft organized, developed paragraphs and use them to construct essays.

**The exercises you will complete in this book are graduated. That means they are arranged in sets of three, called *basic*, *intermediate*, and *challenge*.** The basic drills will often be easy, with simple language on personal topics. The intermediate ones will include somewhat more advanced vocabulary and complicated sentences on campus topics and social issues. The challenge exercises will match the level of English that you will read in your college textbooks and will be expected to write in college courses. The phrasing, vocabulary, and subject matter will be on a higher academic level than in the other exercises.

The exercises are designed to help you understand what you are doing in your own writing by first mastering the basic principles and then applying them to increasingly challenging sentences. Additional exercises at each level are available on the Web if you find yourself needing more work before advancing to the next level. You should go at your own speed and not pass over any of the basic skills you don't fully understand.

Learning the rules of any language takes a lot of practice. So, while you are learning, do plenty of informal writing—pages of it. Do whatever writing your instructor assigns, such as keeping a journal or collecting varied assignments for a portfolio. You should try to develop fluency by doing abundant informal writing while learning to edit and correct your work by reading the explanations and doing the exercises in this book.

## Fluency First: Informal vs. Edited Writing

Informal writing, such as freewriting, e-mail messages, or journal entries, can be of any length and shape. Some people edit their e-mail messages carefully, but many do not, and most do not plan and organize such writing in detail. Such informal writing is like written conversation; it is not expected to be as polished and free of errors as formal speeches, but it is the best way to develop confidence and fluency. While you are learning the patterns of correct, effective English and developing editing skills, your informal writing will help you avoid the hesitation and lack of confidence that can result from worrying about errors. Even though some of your focused writing or journal entries will not be your best work, they will contain original ideas and skillful phrases that you can use later.

Your instructors in courses other than English may want you to write short, informal responses to reading assignments. These will probably be graded more for content than for grammar. Even if such bits of writing are not assigned, you may want to keep a course journal where you write your own summaries of what you learn in each class. Formulating your ideas will help you understand and remember the course material; sometimes it will also force you to confront what you do not understand. Reading your course journal aloud to other students and listening to them read theirs will also help you master course material more thoroughly.

Formal writing, on the other hand, is more like a public speech or a presentation before a committee or class than a conversation. Many writing assignments in college courses will be formal essays, in which the quality of your writing is very important. In some courses, especially advanced ones, you will have to write research papers that will be graded partly on your correct, effective use of language and research format as well as their content. To be well prepared for such advanced work, you should develop proficiency with the basic elements of writing. In this book you will concentrate on using words and sentences correctly in the context of developing, organizing, revising, and proofreading paragraphs. The confidence that you build in learning these skills will prepare you to compose formal assignments in many college courses, and to do other kinds of writing outside your courses, such as reports, business letters, proposals, and possibly even short stories or plays. For that reason, even at the beginning you should become familiar with the stages of the whole writing process.

Philip Eggers
*Borough of Manhattan Community College*
*The City University of New York*

# introduction

## Visualizing the Paragraph in Context

Students in English courses sometimes wonder why they are not doing better, why they are receiving low grades on their assignments or failing writing examinations. "I don't see anything wrong with my writing," some writers say. "What's the problem?"

Often the key problem is the paragraph. Inexperienced writers, even those who can write grammatically and state their ideas clearly, may not develop their paragraphs enough by explaining their ideas in detail and supporting them with examples. What their essays often need is not just more words, or longer sentences, or more paragraphs, but richer, fuller-bodied paragraphs. Their writing may not have obvious errors, but each paragraph may contain only two or three short sentences without much substance. One of the best ways to become a better writer, then, is to learn how to create focused, well-developed paragraphs with varied sentences and interesting content while continuing to raise your level of fluency and correctness. That is what this book is about.

To begin with, visualize your own paragraphs as they might appear in an essay—large building blocks that fill a third of a page or more explaining and illustrating a topic. Rather than rushing through your paragraphs without paying attention to each one, imagine each paragraph as a canvas to be filled with varied forms, colors, and details. Take the time to design, compose, and revise your paragraphs so that the entire composition will be the best you can make it. Of course, no book can give you the blueprint for the many kinds of paragraphs you will write in college. Through practice, however, you can acquire many paragraph skills that will improve the quality of your college essays and any other kind of writing you may do outside college, such as business reports, application letters, or professional writing.

Just what, then, is a paragraph? First of all, paragraphs serve several purposes in a larger work, such as an essay, an article, or a report. Because it is a unit in some larger work, a paragraph may vary in length according to its placement and function in that work. In a college essay, for example, the introductory and concluding paragraphs will usually be shorter than the body paragraphs because their purpose is to move the reader into the main text at the beginning and out of it at the end. The paragraphs we will be working on in *Steps for Writers* will be chiefly body paragraphs, which require clear topics and full development.

To visualize the kinds of paragraphs you will be composing in this book, first imagine the shape of a typical college essay and the way its main parts fit together. Although there are many kinds of essays and many ways of developing them, the chart that follows will give you an overall picture of the most familiar structure for academic essays. The number of paragraphs in an essay will vary according to the length of the essay itself, but most college essays are based on a familiar, logical three-part structure.

## Paragraphs as Building Blocks of Essays

**INTRODUCTION:** Your introduction is a paragraph, or maybe two, that arouses readers' interest in the topic and gives them a clear idea of what you plan to say in the essay. It should begin with a short statement or question that evokes interest, and then continue with several more sentences that lead up to a clear, forceful **thesis statement,** which announces your essay's main point. The thesis statement is often the last sentence in the introduction.

**BODY:** The body of your essay contains several paragraphs, usually three to five, that develop the main point. In this book you will study different ways to develop your points, using description, narration, comparison, persuasion, and so on. Each body paragraph may contain a **topic sentence** that acts as a signpost to guide the reader by introducing the subject of the paragraph. Learning to develop these body paragraphs and connect them with transition words is a major part of learning to write essays.

**CONCLUDING:** Think of the conclusion as your introduction in reverse. You may begin by restating your thesis (though not in exactly the same words). Then find a way to end with interesting statements that leave food for further thought while remaining close to your main idea. Your last sentence, like the first one in your introduction, should be memorable and emphatic—and preferably short.

The diagram above makes it look as if the parts of the essay are just piled on top of one another. But the adventure of writing an essay is not like stacking cans on a grocery store shelf; it is more like exploring a neighborhood—one that you are acquainted with but that also contains many surprises. As you move from one paragraph of your essay to the next, you will say to yourself, "This idea leads me to another point, and that point makes me realize that. . .". An essay is a kind of guided tour from one idea to another. Every paragraph topic should follow from the previous one and every sentence lead to the next. This sequence of ideas and statements is the glue that holds the essay together on the inside and makes the organization of your essay visible to the reader on the outside.

While learning to write paragraphs, then, you should remember that paragraphs must serve as parts of larger compositions. You can improve your writing skills through paragraph practice, but the long-term goal is to create whole essays and other longer compositions. Creating any effective piece of writing, whether a paragraph, an essay, or even a book demands the same skills you will develop while using *Steps for Writers*. Proficient writers have many ways of working, progressing from one stage to another, from their first ideas and prewriting activities through numerous drafts and revisions to a final completed and corrected composition. We call these methods of creating paragraphs and essays the *writing process*, which also involves a process of thinking and learning. As you improve, you will discover the writing process that works best for you.

# Writing Effective Paragraphs

# The Writing Process

---

## STEPPING UP: WRITING TIP 1

There are many different kinds of writing and you may adopt a different process for each kind of writing task you undertake. The elaborate process of prewriting, drafting, revising, and proofreading applies most of all to formal academic writing. Although we generally write memos, greeting card messages, and e-mails spontaneously, most college writing requires more planning and editing. By experimenting, you will be able to develop **the writing process** that works best for you.

---

## Overview of the Writing Process

There are as many writing processes as there are writers. Like all writers, you will find your own way of writing by trial and error. You may like to begin on your computer keyboard, or you may feel comfortable starting out with only a pen or pencil and paper. Like many writers, you may enjoy talking about your ideas and early drafts with someone else—perhaps a group of readers. On the other hand, you may be a thinker and writer who hates to be distracted and does best starting out solo and sharing your work with others only after you have crafted it. At some stage, however, you will almost certainly find others' responses to your work valuable. Your readers will make suggestions you might not have thought of, respond in ways you didn't expect, and give you encouragement about what you do well. Experiment with different approaches and judge by the results. Ask yourself what produces your best writing, not just what method is easiest and most comfortable. Be ready to adopt a method that helps you improve your work.

As different as their individual methods can be, skilled writers share some common practices. Nearly all writers begin with some form of prewriting to explore the subject they are writing about and to organize their material. Next, they create the composition itself, after which they revise what they have written. Finally, they look over their work carefully to correct mistakes. Successful writing almost always develops through these stages, during which some of the work is in the mind and some is written on the page.

While you are studying the lessons and doing the exercises in this book, spend extra time practicing some of the following activities to develop the habit of writing fluently and at length. First, familiarize yourself with the different kinds of prewriting activities.

## Freewriting

**Freewriting** is the act of writing nonstop for several minutes without thinking about errors or corrections, just letting the words flow without interruption. Writers who are troubled with writer's block should practice freewriting in order to gain the kind of fluency in writing they already possess when they converse with friends. Try freewriting yourself to see if you may be unnecessarily blocking your own flow of words.

## Focused Writing

**Focused writing** is much like freewriting except that you try to stay on one main topic—your favorite sport, how you like to dress, a film that you liked, your relationship with your sister. Again, keep writing without stopping. In both freewriting and focused writing, experiment with both writing by hand and typing on a computer to find which method seems to produce a better flow of words for you. If it sounds as though grammar, spelling, punctuation, word choice, and sentence structure are not important, don't be misled—they are. During focused writing and its cousin freewriting, however, you are simply concentrating on something else—getting a lot of words down without too much hesitation. In longer assignments and writing projects, you can deal with the problems of correctness after you have enough writing to edit.

Focused writing can help you continue to increase your fluency while developing the habit of staying on one idea at a time—the primary skill in composing paragraphs and essays. Staying on topic is like staying in your lane when you drive: The idea is simple, but it takes practice to do it consistently.

## Exploring Ideas: Brainstorming and Making Lists

Writing involves thinking as well as putting words down on paper. Certain thinking exercises may help you get started with longer writing assignments when you feel stuck. **Brainstorming** is a word commonly used to describe a session in which you, often with a group, throw out ideas about a topic randomly. If you are going to write about television news, for instance, try spending two or three minutes coming up with everything you can say about that topic. After you have practiced brainstorming on a number of topics, go back to the same topics and write down lists of all the points you can make about them. Then try making some brainstorming lists on new topics, writing down points as they occur to you. To become a stronger writer, you must also become a more active thinker.

## Clustering and Grouping

Brainstorming and listing will allow you to explore the size and range of your topic. The next stage is to see relationships between parts of the topic, to sort out the main ideas from supporting ideas and facts. **Clustering** is a technique in which you arrange a main idea in the center with supporting ideas branching off from it, like this:

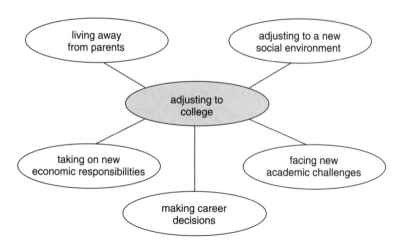

Another method of moving beyond list-making is to survey a list you have made and number the items in four or five categories. This procedure will help you sort out your ideas in a logical fashion before you write a complete draft of your essay.

## Organizing, Outlining, and Composing

The composing you will do in this book will concentrate mostly on paragraph construction. You will be working on methods of organizing paragraphs. Remember, however, that college writing will involve essays that usually range from a few pages to ten pages or more for research papers. What you are working on in this book is part of a larger whole built on words, sentences, and paragraphs; therefore, you will need word, sentence, and paragraph mastery to be ready to compose these larger assignments. In the process of putting together a whole essay, you may find it helpful to use a formal outline, dividing your topic into categories and each category into specific supporting points and examples. Here is one possible outline on the topic of adjusting to college.

Main idea: Attending college requires several kinds of adjustment.

I. Social adjustments
   A. Living away from parents
   B. Joining clubs and organizations
   C. Meeting more diverse friends and acquaintances
   D. Developing romantic relationships
II. Intellectual adjustments
   A. Learning to think for oneself
   B. Studying new subjects
   C. Being influenced by other students' ideas
III. Personal adjustments
   A. Managing finances
   B. Making career decisions
   C. Balancing work and extracurricular activities

As you work at writing paragraphs, remember that each paragraph fits into a larger essay. In an essay based on the outline above, for example, each subtopic would require at least one paragraph of discussion, possibly more.

## Editing and Proofreading

The last stages of the writing process are **editing** and **proofreading.** When you edit and proofread, you examine your work several times, checking for errors in the grammatical structure of your sentences and in spelling, capitalization, and punctuation. In this book you will primarily work on the mastery of words, sentences, and paragraphs so that as you explore the whole writing process and produce longer pieces of writing, you will be confident that you are using acceptable English. You will not be able to edit and proofread effectively unless you understand the do's and don'ts of words, sentences, and paragraphs. And it will not do much good to learn everything in this book if you don't make use of your new knowledge and skills by proofreading your work carefully. It is important to learn the guidelines that govern written expression in English and then to apply what you have learned.

## Writing Assignments and Activities to Get Started

### Keeping a Journal

To become more fluent, write something every day. Keep a journal in which you write at least a page or two on anything that interests you. This journal may give you topics and ideas to use in creating paragraphs or other formal writing assignments in your course. Your journal should allow you to write comfortably and quickly, concentrating on the topic and your ideas about it. Note: This activity is especially important if you haven't done much writing in school or haven't been in school for years. Many students who avoid writing because they don't know how to get started turn out to be exceptional writers. A few have even become well-known authors.

Keeping a journal is not quite the same as keeping a diary. Your journal should be a rich source of ideas for larger and more formal compositions, not a secret and private account of the intimate details of your life. Use your journal to reflect on articles you read, programs you see on television or hear on the radio, events that occur around you, and activities in which you participate. Your journal should be a record of your responses to your environment and a means of examining your life. It should also be a vehicle for using writing as a mode of thinking and expressing ideas. Your journal may serve many uses besides writing practice, such as psychological growth and academic empowerment, but its primary value should be that it makes you a better writer.

## Topics for Journal Entries

Try to focus on an interesting topic every time you make an entry in your journal. If you do that, you will learn to develop ideas more extensively, and your journal will be a great resource for essay topics.

**Basic Topics.** Eating well, living with a pet, managing money, using your cell phone, using e-mail, communicating on FaceBook, listening to your favorite music, watching your favorite TV program, using a credit card, taking a trip, having an argument with someone in your family.

**Intermediate Topics.** Becoming a parent, caring for a child, choosing a career, learning a foreign language, defending your opinion about why you should or should not vote, describing two public figures and explaining how they differ, explaining what causes some people to succeed despite their disadvantages, identifying the effects of the commercialization of sports, enumerating the qualities of a great film, explaining the appeal of reality TV shows.

**Challenge Topics.** Summarizing an interesting newspaper article and explaining your opinions about the topic, reading a poem or story and explaining what the author means and what the work means to you, summarizing a passage from a textbook you are reading and telling what this passage says to you, visiting an exhibit, performance, public reading, play, or museum and explaining what it means to you.

# Using a Computer Along with This Book

You will probably have many opportunities to use computers in a lab or at home; working with the exercises accompanying the book, you can reinforce what you learn in the classroom. If your class already meets in a computer lab, you will certainly want to extend your work beyond the book to the exercises available. **Online exercises will allow you to do additional practice at each level whenever you find yourself not quite confident enough to proceed to the next level.**

mywritinglab

If your class is using this book, you may use exercises provided at the Longman Web site: www.mycomplab.com/.

In addition, most major universities sponsor Web sites, usually called "owls" (short for online writing labs), which can give you both guidance and skill-building exercises in grammar, composition, and research. Two well-known online writing labs are the City University of New York lab (CUNY Write Site) at http://writesite.cuny.edu and the Purdue OWL at http://owl.english.Purdue.edu. These labs and others like them offer many additional online writing resources such as quizzes, practice sets, dictionaries, encyclopedias, collections of literary works, and lists of other university online writing labs. Your college is very likely to have online writing resources of its own; be sure to ask your instructor. However, you should be sure that the online resources at your college are up to date and reflect the current testing requirements.

The pervasive use of computers in both school and the workplace raises the question of whether to compose longhand or at the keyboard. This may be a choice available to you, or it may not. If you face a basic skills examination that must be written with pen and paper, it may be impractical to do all of your composing on a computer keyboard. On the other hand, it is highly impractical in the long run to avoid the keyboard, as today nearly all writing—including college writing—is done in a word-processing format. Some writers still strongly prefer to compose their first drafts in script. If you find yourself better able to think with a pen or pencil in your hand, don't let technology stand in your way. Do what works for you when you compose. However, you must be ready to present revised and copyedited final drafts in your courses and, when necessary, on the job. When you compose at the keyboard, use spelling checks and grammar checks as often as you can, but remember that they can help you only if you develop a good command of grammar and spelling.

## Key Words from Chapter 1 for Review

brainstorming, clustering, editing, focused writing, freewriting, proofreading, the writing process, topics

# CHAPTER 2

# Paragraph Basics

---

STEPPING UP: WRITING TIP 2

Not all the paragraphs in a book, magazine, or newspaper you are reading will resemble the ones you write in these exercises. Not every paragraph has an obvious topic sentence, and paragraphs vary widely in length. Newspaper paragraphs are often short; paragraphs in academic journals are usually very long. Some professional writers like long, elaborate paragraphs; others prefer short ones with a lot of punch. Nevertheless, for college writing you will need the ability to create standard-size paragraphs that have clear, fully developed topics, usually stated at the beginning. Once you have mastered basic paragraph skills, you will be able to vary your paragraph strategies the way professional writers often do.

---

## Writing Assignment: Creating Paragraphs

One key to writing well is to learn how to write paragraphs effectively. Notice your paragraphs—**indent** them properly, develop them well, and make sure they stay on topic. When you do prewriting and develop drafts, you may not pay much attention to your paragraphs. But once you have created a draft—whether it is an essay, a report, a letter, or a research paper—be sure to look at all your paragraphs carefully. Can the reader readily grasp the purpose of every paragraph? Does each paragraph fulfill its purpose? Does each paragraph follow logically from the one that precedes it?

To learn how to create successful paragraphs, you will need to work with some samples of your own paragraphs. To get the "feel" of writing paragraphs, choose five of the following subjects and write a focused paragraph on each one. Try to stay on topic and develop your ideas without wandering off.

- Tell about a responsibility you chose to accept and explain how well you met it.
- Write a paragraph in which you express an opinion about a course you have taken.
- Write a paragraph in which you describe one of your own best qualities.
- Write a paragraph explaining how college turned out to be different than you expected.
- Write a paragraph in which you explain why you do or do not want to remain in the city or town where you now reside.
- Write a paragraph beginning with the statement, "The college I attend could be improved by . . .".
- Write a paragraph beginning with the statement, "The best way to lose weight is . . .".
- Write a paragraph summarizing an editorial in a newspaper.

## MODEL PARAGRAPHS

Read each model paragraph below and answer the questions that follow it.

## Model Paragraph: Basic Level

Alan and his sister Yvonne are similar in many ways, but their shopping patterns are different because of their lifestyles. Alan likes to shop at large discount and wholesale stores like Wal-Mart and Costco, but his sister Yvonne buys everything at small neighborhood groceries, pharmacies, and clothing stores. Alan, who drives a large SUV and lives with his family in a two-story house in the suburbs, insists that he saves a lot of money by buying in bulk, bringing home huge packages of paper towels, underwear, and soda. He buys tools, electrical equipment, CDs, books, and holiday cards in large quantities. Yvonne doesn't have room in her small apartment to store large packages, and she doesn't have a car to travel to the mall, so she likes to shop on her block. She also insists that Alan buys superfluous things, and that he doesn't save as much money as she does by being more selective. Besides, she says, she enjoys picking out individual items and trying different brands. Although Alan insists that the service at the outlets where he shops is very efficient and the workers are polite, Yvonne believes that the personal relationships she has developed with retailers in her neighborhood often give her special benefits. Her pharmacist can get her discounts on prescription drugs and cosmetics, and the woman in the clothing store where she shops knows exactly what will fit her and look good on her. Alan doesn't agree; he says he knows what he wants, he saves money, and his family never runs out of supplies.

1. Explain the meaning of the following terms: *discount, wholesale, superfluous, retailers.*
2. What is the purpose of this paragraph?
3. Which sentence states the overall point of the paragraph?
4. Does the author favor one method of shopping over the other? Explain your response.
5. How do Alan's and Yvonne's lifestyles influence their shopping patterns?
6. What details are mentioned that give examples of shopping patterns?
7. Would you categorize this paragraph as a narrative, description, argument, or comparison?

## Model Paragraph: Intermediate Level

More guns were fired, and people broke into every direction. Not knowing where I could find safety, I just ran as fast as possible, following a young woman before me. She looked like a college teacher or a graduate student, wearing bobbed hair, brass-rimmed glasses, and a pastel dress with accordion pleats. As we were approaching a tall billboard, a volley of gunfire swept down a few people ahead of me. The young woman fell, then scrambled to her feet and zigzagged forward, shrieking, with both hands holding her bleeding left side. One of her shoes was missing, and her white stockings were soaked with blood. I pulled her aside to keep her from being trampled. She dropped down, but I dared not stop to carry her away because more bullets whizzed by, drawing blazing lines. I fled with the crowd, running and running until we ended in a small alley. My heart was beating so violently that I couldn't help trembling.

—Ha Jin, *The Crazed* (New York: Vintage, 2002), 304.

1. Explain the meaning of the following terms: *bobbed hair, pastel, accordion pleats, volley.*
2. What details describing the young woman create a sense of panic?
3. What action words (verbs) create a sense of violence and excitement? What effect is created by the use of verbs ending in *ing* (*shrieking, running*)?
4. What descriptive details make the young woman seem out of place in a scene of violence?
5. How would you describe the actions of the narrator (the young man telling the story)?
6. What words appeal to the senses of sight, hearing, and touch?
7. Imagine you are making a movie of this scene, which takes place during the protest at Tiananmen Square in 1989. How would the camera move from one shot to the next in order to capture everything referred to in the paragraph?

## Model Paragraph: Challenge Level

The computer cannot think; it cannot act; it has no volition or purpose; but there is an eerie economy of effect in its operations and a genius of a singular order in its design, a form of cunning commanded by no other intellectual instrument. It achieves its striking results by simplifying its organization so that it encompasses a few basic logical operations. It addresses a world presented in chunks of data and by virtue of its great speed and simplicity manages to coordinate aspects of that world *directly*, with no mediation of theory, no appeal to abstract concepts. The computer maintains no contact with the concepts of continuity. It is supremely an instrument by which connections are tracked in time and then recorded. If the calculus embodies, or at least represents, an ancient human urge toward theoretical abstraction, the computer represents, and may embody, an equally ancient human urge toward factual mastery.

—David Berlinski, *A Tour of the Calculus* (New York: Vintage, 1995), 308.

1. Explain the meaning of the following words and phrases: *volition, economy of effect, mediation of theory, embodies, urge toward theoretical abstraction.*
2. What does the author say about computers?
3. What does the author say about calculus? What is the difference between computers and calculus?
4. How does the author develop the main idea of this paragraph?
5. Why does he not use any concrete examples?
6. Is the author's purpose to present facts, tell a story, or express an opinion? Explain your response.
7. What, if anything, do you agree with in this paragraph? What, if anything, do you disagree with in this paragraph?

# Paragraph Unity

A paragraph that has **unity** has one clear purpose. In each of the paragraphs above, every sentence is closely connected to the same overall idea. Examine the paragraphs you wrote in the activity you completed earlier (Writing Assignment, Creating Paragraphs), and see if you stayed on topic for each from beginning to end. In an effective paragraph, the topic is limited enough so that the rest of the paragraph can support it well, and no statements wander off the topic. When you compose paragraphs, you will have to pay close attention to identifying your topic, stating it in a topic sentence, usually at the beginning, and developing it without digressing. Every sentence in your paragraph should follow logically from the one before it, and all sentences should give facts, ideas, or examples that support the topic statement.

---

## TEST YOURSELF: Paragraph Unity

Practice recognizing sentences that support a topic and those that do not. First read the topic sentence; then read each of the seven sentences that follow. If the sentence supports the topic statement, write S in the blank next to it. If it is off topic, write O in the space; if it negates the topic statement, write N in the space.

**Topic statement:** Marcela is good at multitasking.

_____ 1. Marcela can talk on her cell phone and read a textbook at the same time.

_____ 2. Marcela can translate Spanish into English while watching television.

_____ 3. Marcela has difficulty cooking several dishes at the same time.

_____ 4. Marcela once had an accident because she was texting while driving.

_____ 5. Marcela can carry on conversations with three customers at the same time.

_____ 6. Marcella attends a community college.

_____ 7. Marcella can listen to a lecture while drawing sketches of her classmates.

*Answers:* 1. S 2. S 3. N 4. N 5. S 6. O 7. S

WRITING EXERCISES: Basic, Intermediate, Challenge

## Basic Exercise: Paragraph Unity

This exercise will give you practice in recognizing sentences that support a topic. First read the topic sentence; then read each of the seven sentences that follow it. If the sentence supports the topic statement, write S in the blank next to it. If it is off topic, write O in the space; if it negates the topic statement, write N in the space.

**Topic statement:** Karen is an obsessive person.

_____ 1. Karen counts the words in all of her essays.

_____ 2. Karen enunciates every syllable when she reads aloud.

_____ 3. Karen grew up in Michigan.

_____ 4. Karen's handwriting is extremely neat and even.

_____ 5. Karen can't stand to make one mistake on her quizzes.

_____ 6. Karen enjoys playing the guitar.

_____ 7. Karen doesn't pay attention in class.

## Intermediate Exercise: Paragraph Unity

**Topic statement:** Participating in college sports has educational value.

_____ 1. Students who participate in college sports are popular.

_____ 2. Sports teach students effective team thinking.

_____ 3. Athletes are required to maintain satisfactory grade point averages.

_____ 4. Student athletes carry over the spirit of supportive competition to their course work.

_____ 5. Most athletes spend so much time in training they can't do well in their courses.

6. Baseball is less of a spectator sport in college than football and basketball.

7. Coping with success and failure in sports is a learning process that applies to academic work.

## Challenge Exercise: Paragraph Unity

**Topic statement:** Writing well requires the mastery of different skills.

_____ 1. Writing requires an advanced knowledge of grammar and syntax.

_____ 2. Writing is being introduced into elementary school curricula throughout the country.

_____ 3. Writing is an important but narrow skill unrelated to any others.

_____ 4. Personal writing requires the ability to recall the details of an experience.

_____ 5. Visualization is an important part of descriptive writing.

_____ 6. Some people have succeeded and become famous without being able to write well.

_____ 7. Writing effectively requires shrewd critical thinking.

# Using Topic Sentences to Guide Your Reader

Learn to use topic sentences and unified paragraphs to guide your reader. Not every paragraph must begin by announcing its purpose. However, in order to develop the habit of using paragraphs effectively, you should practice writing paragraphs that do begin with topic sentences containing key words that will help the reader understand your purpose. Like signs on a thruway, topic sentences must give clear directions. A sign that says "New York 90 Miles" or "Exit 32, Baltimore" tells the driver what's on the road ahead. A topic sentence that says, "My aunt has old-fashioned ideas" tips off the reader about what to expect in the whole paragraph.

## Basic Sample Paragraph

### Topic Sentence

_My aunt has old-fashioned ideas._ She thinks that young people should dress conservatively and go to church every Sunday. She believes that teenagers should not date before they are sixteen years old and should never go out on dates without an adult accompanying them. According to her, girls should act quiet and polite. She doesn't believe that anyone should have sex before getting married. She thinks women should just get married, raise lots of children, and not work outside the home. She can't stand to hear people curse, and the music her nephews and nieces listen to she considers trash. Most of all, she cannot bear to witness young people disrespecting their elders.

Imagine that paragraph without the topic sentence. The reader would keep asking, "What's the point? What's the point?" Smart readers might figure out the point by the end of the paragraph, but you shouldn't keep them guessing. An effective **topic sentence** at the beginning of a paragraph makes clear to the reader the point of the paragraph. Read the two paragraphs that follow and explain the relationship between the topic sentence and the rest of the paragraph.

## Intermediate Sample Paragraph

### Topic Sentence

Current fashions in clothing are extremely adaptable. People once thought that they had to adapt to the latest fashions in clothes even if they were uncomfortable or inconvenient. Nowadays most people believe that their own comfort comes first and that fashions should adjust to their needs. In many situations that once called for formal clothing, such as at business offices, courtrooms, concert halls, and theaters, some people dress informally rather than in suits and long dresses. It has even become fashionable to have "casual Fridays" in businesses, and people at some jobs even wear casual clothes all week long. "Business casual," or what the British call "smart casual," has become a standard for tourists, employees, and even managers. Meanwhile, the traditional range of long dresses, business suits, and formal wear is still available for occasions such as graduations, weddings, and other ceremonies where people want to appear in fine apparel. While it wouldn't be quite accurate to say that "anything goes," there is great flexibility in today's fashions.

## Challenge Sample Paragraph

### Topic Sentence

The exploration of Mars has more benefits than drawbacks. Attempts to send spacecraft to Mars have just as often met with failure as with success, and the expenditures for these ventures in money and *scientific expertise are very high. Some people might argue that the planet seems to be more barren than the deserts on earth and therefore not worth exploring; however, it is exciting to find out everything we can about the planet that most resembles Earth—that is, Earth as it was billions of years ago—in the effort to learn whether extraterrestrial life has ever existed. In addition, the coordination of such space projects is resulting in improved technology in areas such as robotics, photography, and communications. In the process of exploring Mars we are also discovering much about the behavior of materials in extreme temperatures, the reception of extremely faint signals by radio telescopes, and the effect of erosion on varied landscapes. We are hoping to learn significant truths about our own origins and the origin of life itself, and, finally, by exploring Mars we may make discoveries in areas we do not expect—which often happens during any search into the unknown. Although the cost of the Mars projects is high, we will inevitably be spending large sums on space exploration of some kind, and a thorough knowledge of Mars is one of its most attractive and promising objectives. The cost is not exorbitant, and the benefits may repay the expenditure many times over.*

A topic sentence is the one that says, "This is what this paragraph is going to discuss." It charts the direction and boundaries of the paragraph. It should be just broad enough to include all the other sentences in the paragraph, but not too broad. If the topic sentence is too general, it will draw boundaries too wide for a paragraph to fill. If the topic sentence is too narrow and factual, it will fail to draw any boundaries for the rest of the paragraph.

Can you tell the difference between a broad statement and a limited statement? Which of the following three statements is broadest? Which is most limited?

1. The leading actress in this film gave a stunning performance.
2. This film was released on March 1, 2011.
3. There were many outstanding films last year.

Only one of these would make an effective topic sentence for a paragraph.

Statement 3 is too broad for a single paragraph: discussing all films made last year would take up more than a paragraph.

Statement 2 is merely a factual statement; it leads nowhere.

Statement 1 might make a good topic sentence because it is broad enough to include a number of supporting facts but limited enough to be discussed in a paragraph. It could serve as a guide, leading the reader to expect examples of what the actress did well.

---

## TEST YOURSELF: Topic Sentences

If the following sentences were in the same paragraph,

A. Find one sentence that would make a good topic sentence that includes all the others.
B. Find one sentence that is not on topic and would not belong in the same paragraph.

1. Reading appeals to Evan more than going to parties.
2. Evan likes to communicate on Facebook more than in person.
3. Evan took a trip to Chicago last month.
4. Evan is a shy person.
5. Evan doesn't like to give oral reports in class.
6. Evan wears conservative clothes so that he won't be noticed.
7. Evan is not comfortable around strangers.

*Answers:* Sentence 4 is the topic sentence. Sentence 3 is not relevant to the topic. All the others support the topic.

---

## WRITING EXERCISES: Basic, Intermediate, Challenge

# Basic Exercise: Topic Sentences

If the following sentences were in the same paragraph,

A. Find one sentence that would make a good topic sentence that includes all the others.
B. Find one sentence that is not on topic and would not belong in the same paragraph.

1. Melanie drives fast and honks at other drivers to get out of the way.
2. When she doesn't like what other people say, Melanie usually tells them off.
3. In debate tournaments, Melanie intimidates her opponents.
4. Melanie is a very aggressive person.
5. In her college classes, Melanie talks more than anyone else.
6. Melanie bargains with street vendors and usually gets the prices she wants.
7. Melanie grew up in a suburb of Cincinnati.

## Intermediate Exercise: Topic Sentences

If the following sentences were in the same paragraph,

A. Find one sentence that would make a good topic sentence that includes all the others.
B. Find one sentence that is not on topic and would not belong in the same paragraph.

1. Most large retail businesses offer their products online.
2. It is easy to compare the quality and prices of products online.
3. Shopping online offers many advantages.
4. Online customers can buy products not sold in their local stores.
5. Online purchases require customers to fill in complicated forms and supply credit information.
6. Shoppers can read the online reports of satisfied and dissatisfied customers.
7. Visual images of products are often available online.

## Challenge Exercise: Topic Sentences

If the following sentences were in the same paragraph,

A. Find one sentence that would make a good topic sentence that includes all the others.
B. Find one sentence that is not on topic and would not belong in the same paragraph.

1. Many exquisite artifacts and pieces of sculpture from Petra have been preserved.
2. The water system of Petra was a marvel of early engineering.
3. Petra was once a center of trade for the entire Middle East.
4. Tourists find it too hot to visit Petra in the summer.
5. The lost city of Petra in Jordan is fascinating to study about for many reasons.
6. The effects of a major earthquake in Petra make an interesting ecological study.
7. Petra shows cultural influences of the Roman Empire, Byzantium, and Islam.

## Basic Exercise II: Topic Sentences

Do a prewriting exercise of your own choosing (focused writing, clustering, brainstorming, and so on) about your own neighborhood.

Then look over your material and find a **key idea**. Write this idea in the form of a topic sentence. List as many supporting details as you can. Write a paragraph of about 150 words beginning with the topic sentence you composed. Be sure to stay on topic!

## Intermediate Exercise II: Topic Sentences

Do a prewriting exercise of your own choosing (focused writing, clustering, brainstorming, and so on) about an issue that is in the news. Then look over your material and find a key idea. Write this idea in the form of a topic sentence. List as many supporting details as you can. Write a paragraph of about 150 words beginning with the topic sentence you composed. Be sure to stay on topic!

## Challenge Exercise II: Topic Sentences

Do a prewriting exercise of your own choosing (focused writing, clustering, brainstorming, and so on) about a topic you have just studied in a content course such as history, economics, computer science, or art history. Then look over your material and find a key idea. Write this idea in the form of a topic sentence. List as many supporting details as you can. Write a paragraph of about 150 words beginning with the topic sentence you composed. Be sure to stay on topic!

## Basic Exercise III: Topic Sentences

Read the paragraph that follows, noting all the supporting points. Then write a topic sentence for the paragraph in the blank.

_____.

Luke usually showed up late to class, often without his book. Whenever he was supposed to write, he had to borrow a pen and paper from another student. His cell phone often went off during the class, and he would carry on conversations in the back of the room while the teacher was talking. He didn't usually do his assignments, and on the day of an important test he was sure to be absent. He turned papers in late, and he never proofread them before handing them in. When he was supposed to work with other students in a small group, he often took out a sports magazine and began reading it. When he did speak in class, he usually brought up a subject unrelated to the class discussion. The weekend before the final examination he spent on a trip to the city with his friends, and he showed up for the exam barely able to keep his eyes open. Nobody was surprised when he failed the course.

## Intermediate Exercise III: Topic Sentences

Read the paragraph that follows, noting all the supporting points. Then write a topic sentence for the paragraph in the blank.

_____. One weight loss program eliminates most fatty foods, especially red meat and cheese, from the diet while reducing the total number of daily calories a person takes in. Another approach sends daily packages to your door containing all the food you should eat for that day, and it isn't very much. Still other diets almost eliminate carbohydrates but allow the dieter to eat red meat and other fatty foods, though in limited amounts. Most diets require the person to be very moderate about eating high-calorie desserts or to eliminate them altogether, and, while they disagree about how much snacking a person can do, none of them allow a person to just eat as much as he or she wants.

## Challenge Exercise III: Topic Sentences

Read the paragraph that follows, noting all the supporting points. Then write a topic sentence for the paragraph in the blank.

_____. Tests such as the SAT and ACT are intended to measure high school students' thinking ability. Not only are these tests open to cultural biases, but they also do not take into account the many kinds of functioning the mind is capable of, from understanding social relationships to identifying musical tones. Such tests do not account for the way a person reacts to the pressure of a test-taking situation. They do not measure differences in motivation. How can we tell, for instance, whether a person who doesn't care about getting a high score will perform as well as he or she is capable of doing? Although these tests measure a kind of analytical thinking, they do not give a picture of the person's learning style, and they do not say much about the person's learning development over a period of years or the amount of knowledge the person possesses. Finally, they do not tell how the person applies his or her intelligence in everyday life, which may have as much to do with success in college and careers as test scores do.

# Using Key Words in Topic Sentences

A topic sentence does more than just name a subject. It expresses an opinion about the subject; it points a direction, opens a discussion, and creates an impression of the subject. A simple statement of fact, such as "It is raining outside," does not make a useful topic sentence. Which of these two might make an effective topic sentence?

A. I have a friend named Sarah.
B. My friend Sarah is very persistent.

Suppose you wanted to describe Sarah and began with sentence A. What would that sentence describe about Sarah? The reader would have no specific idea. Sentence B makes a better topic statement because it tells the reader what to expect: You are going to explain how persistent Sarah is. What examples of behavior might show how persistent she is? *Persistent* is the **key word** in sentence B. It introduces a controlling idea. Most good topic sentences contain such a key word or phrase.

Compare these statements:

A. Superior College offers *technologically innovative* business courses.
B. Superior College is a *good* place to study.

*Good* is one of those catchall terms, like *nice, bad, interesting, great,* and *unique,* that lead anywhere or nowhere in particular. The first statement makes a specific point that the writer must then support with specific facts. What technological innovations can you think of that would make effective examples in a paragraph beginning with Sentence A?

### TEST YOURSELF: Key Words

In the following sentences, underline the key words or phrases that create specific impressions. Identify any statements that would not make effective topic sentences because they lack specific key words or phrases.

1. Inez is an ambitious person.
2. Russell thought it was a good game.
3. The book had a complicated plot.
4. The film was historically accurate.
5. Sofia found it convenient to live near the campus.
6. The job taught Eduardo managerial skills.
7. The restaurant has a really nice décor.

*Answers:* Key words and phrases: 1. Ambitious 2. *good* is too vague 3. complicated 4. historically accurate 5. convenient 6. managerial skills 7. *nice* is too vague

## Basic Exercise: Key Words

In each sentence, identify the key word or phrase that creates a plan for a paragraph. Identify any statements that would not succeed as topic sentences because they lack effective key words or phrases. Supply effective key words or phrases where they are lacking.

1. My first cooking lesson was a surprising experience.
2. Stephen is a hypocritical friend.
3. The commencement ceremony was emotionally inspiring.
4. Our visit to Florida was nice.
5. Adjusting to the new coach was frustrating for the team.
6. Jennifer's boyfriend is okay.
7. Alex gave unconvincing excuses for not doing the work.

## Intermediate Exercise: Key Words

In each sentence, identify the key word or phrase that creates a plan for a paragraph. Identify any statements that would not succeed as topic sentences because they lack effective key words or phrases. Supply effective key words or phrases where they are lacking.

1. Alexander's imitation of Glenn Beck is hilarious.
2. The team is better prepared for the tournament this year than it was last year.
3. The readings in the course are no good.
4. The news media portray Lady Gaga as a narcissistic person.
5. The job description seems to call for a versatile employee.
6. Undocumented immigrants are numerous.
7. The landscape created an impression of mystery.

## Challenge Exercise: Key Words

In each sentence, identify the key word or phrase that creates a plan for a paragraph. Identify any statements that would not succeed as topic sentences because they lack effective key words or phrases. Supply effective key words or phrases where they are lacking.

1. The poem is filled with ambiguities.
2. The argument lacks a theoretical basis.
3. The statistical report is filled with errors in computation.

4. The thesis of the paper is interesting.
5. The final plans for the memorial differ significantly from the original proposal.
6. The antiquity of the site was confirmed by several kinds of scientific analysis.
7. The increase in retail sales during the spring confirmed experts' predictions.

---

## Basic Writing Assignment: Key Words

Think about someone you know who has an unusual personality trait. Brainstorm for ten minutes, listing everything you can think of about how this person talks, thinks, and behaves. Then look over the list and find one main point that you can make about this person—a point that will include most of the details you have listed. Eliminate the details that do not fit this point. Write a topic sentence using a key word or phrase, such as *eccentric, ambitious, artistic, public-spirited, egotistical, altruistic,* or *spiritual,* to describe this person. Compose an exploratory draft of a paragraph describing this person. Look over your draft to be sure that all sentences support the topic and that the whole paragraph reads smoothly. Make revisions and write a final draft.

### Sample Paragraph

Read this paragraph to help you brainstorm your topic. What is the key word describing Isabella? Notice how the student who wrote this paragraph succeeded in stating a clear topic sentence and developing it in an interesting way. Try to make your final draft equally unified and interesting.

> *Isabella is an unusually self-sacrificing person. In her job as a licensed practical nurse, she works many hours, sometimes twelve hours in one day, helping poor people with their problems. She helps deliver babies and works in the emergency room, where she assists in caring for people with heart attacks and many other medical problems. She often calls these people after they leave the hospital to see how they are doing and has made friends with many of the families she has helped. She also cares for her 91-year-old aunt who is not able to go out anymore and is barely able to see. Isabella has already*

*raised two daughters and a son, and all of them are going to college or graduate school, but she still keeps track of everything they do, even though they tell her to do more for herself. But her philosophy is to help others first, and she will always do that.*

## Intermediate Writing Assignment: Key Words

Think about an experience you had that can be described by a single key word or phrase such as *hilarious, frightening, heartbreaking, inspiring,* or, better yet, a key word of your own. Compose an exploratory draft of a paragraph telling what happened, emphasizing the details that illustrate your key word. Look over your draft to be sure that all sentences are on topic and that the whole paragraph reads smoothly. Make revisions, adding details where necessary and eliminating irrelevant statements. Write a final draft.

### Sample Paragraph

Read this paragraph to help you brainstorm your topic. What is the key word that characterizes the experience? Notice how the student who wrote this paragraph succeeded in stating a clear topic sentence and developing it in an interesting way. Try to make your final draft equally unified and interesting.

*Applying to colleges was a frustrating experience for me. My high school counselor told me during my junior year that I had to start researching colleges and taking a lot of tests. I tried looking up some nearby colleges on the Web, but most of them were too expensive and didn't offer the major I wanted, which was exercise physiology. I took the PSATs and didn't do as well as I expected, so my counselor told me to apply in my senior year to a state college. I took the SATs and did a little better than the year before, so I applied to the state college. I filled out all the forms and wrote a long essay about why I wanted to go to that college, but I was put on their waiting list. Then I applied to two private colleges and was admitted to one of them but did not get enough financial aid to go there without taking on a big debt. Finally, I found out about a program in exercise physiology in my local community college and decided to do that instead. Unfortunately, the program was filled for that semester, so I had to enroll as a liberal arts major for one semester and then enter the program later. As frustrating as it all was, I'm happy with the program, and it all turned out well.*

# Challenge Writing Assignment: Key Words

Think of a social issue that you have strong feelings about, such as immigration, the death penalty, abortion, prayer in the schools, health care, unemployment, the media in politics, or terrorism. Write a topic sentence expressing your opinion about the issue using a key word or phrase, such as *beneficial, harmful, fair, unfair, effective, ineffective, unconstitutional, forward-looking,* or *obsolete.* Compose an exploratory draft of a paragraph explaining your opinion. Look over your draft to be sure that all sentences are on topic and that the whole paragraph reads smoothly. Make revisions, adding explanations or examples where needed and eliminating irrelevant statements. Write a final draft.

## Sample Paragraph

Read this paragraph to help you brainstorm your topic. What is the key word the writer uses to explain her opinion on the issue? Notice how the student who wrote this paragraph succeeded in stating a clear topic sentence and developing it in an interesting way. Try to make your final draft equally unified and interesting.

*Passing and enforcing stricter laws against illegal immigration would not be effective. The laws we have are already strict enough, and we have trouble enforcing them. If we were to punish undocumented workers even more harshly and add more guards to prevent people from crossing the border, it would be very expensive and even prevent many farms and businesses from hiring the help they need. These workers take jobs that other people do not want, and they work very hard. Cracking down on them would hurt the economy and cost the government money at a time when there is already a budget problem. Furthermore, no increase in border security can prevent visitors from countries all over the world from overstaying their visas and becoming undocumented. Spending more government money and passing tougher laws to prevent such visitors from staying would just make our fiscal problems worse and deprive the country of valuable people who might become productive citizens. More effective methods of dealing with illegal immigration are needed, such as a guest worker program that would allow workers to stay while still ensuring that the United States has a right to control its immigration.*

## Key Words from Chapter 2 for Review

indent, key idea, key words, topic sentence, unity

# CHAPTER 3

# Qualities of Effective Paragraphs

---

### STEPPING UP: WRITING TIP 3

Developing your paragraphs richly is a key to effective writing. Beginning writers who constantly get stuck and never seem to have enough to say can usually benefit from paragraph practice. Such writers may start an essay, write for a few minutes, put down the pen, and think, "That's all I have to say." Usually what they have written is in bite-size paragraphs of one or two sentences, each of which could be elaborated much further. If you really explain and illustrate what you have to say in each paragraph, making it six, seven, or eight sentences long, you will not find it difficult to complete a 500-word essay.

---

## Paragraph Development

Along with having a clear topic and unity, a paragraph must also be adequately developed. **Paragraph development** does not just mean length. A long paragraph that wanders off the topic or is repetitious, for instance, may be less developed than one that is not quite so long but is rich in supporting details. Development means supporting the topic statement with examples, quotations, explanations, facts, statistics, descriptive details, and ideas. There are many kinds of paragraph development, as we will see.

Inexperienced writers often do not realize how much supporting material they need, and they tend to write underdeveloped paragraphs. Be ambitious and overdo it a little; you can always remove material that you don't need. Here, for instance, is the rough draft of a paragraph that gives only a sketchy idea of the topic.

*Lady Gaga makes original and creative use of techniques developed by previous popular music stars and adds her own distinctive elements. It is easy to see the influence of earlier singers and dancers on her albums, but she has her own way of reaching modern audiences.*

Although this paragraph stays on the topic, it does not say much about it. A reader is likely to feel cheated and to want more details. In this revised draft there is plenty of interesting detail.

*Lady Gaga makes original and creative use of techniques and styles developed by previous popular music stars and adds her own distinctive elements. Her resemblance to Madonna is obvious: A young woman with strict Catholic education, like Madonna she flaunts her sexuality and defies traditional morality in hits like "Born That Way." Her dancing and video imagery show influences of both Madonna and Michael Jackson, and the transformations of her personal image could not have happened without the example of David Bowie. Influences of Elton John and Queen on her music are also detectable, and the rhymes and rhythm of hip-hop are evident in her music, as in the work of most of today's popular artists. Her outfits are also influenced by the extreme fashions of modern clothing designers like Donatella Versace and Alexander McQueen. By incorporating elements of these previous styles and techniques into a new art form all her own, she has attained enormous worldwide popularity. Her fans would say that although she has done more borrowing than any other star, she has made more original use of her material than anyone else.*

How much development is enough? No rules will tell you. Every paragraph is different, and every paragraph is part of a larger piece of writing. Some paragraphs are nine or ten sentences long, and some only one or two. Your purpose as expressed in the topic sentence will determine how much detail you should put into the paragraph. You can tell whether your paragraphs are developed enough by putting your work aside and reading it a few days later. Imagine it is someone else's writing and you are reading it for the first time. Does the paragraph say enough about the topic? To be sure, read your work aloud to someone else and get his or her response.

## Basic Exercise: Paragraph Development

The following paragraph is too short; it stays on the topic but lacks development. Rewrite the paragraph, adding details that help the reader visualize how you dress and the situations you are often in. Replace vague words with specific ones that describe your clothing and your activities.

### Undeveloped Paragraph

The way I dress depends on the circumstances. When I am in casual situations, I wear informal clothes that suit my taste. When I am ready for action, I wear whatever seems attractive and comfortable for doing my favorite activities. For more formal situations, I put on clothes that give me the look I want.

## Intermediate Exercise: Paragraph Development

The following paragraph is too short; it stays on the topic but lacks development. Begin by replacing the key words "quite an experience" with a more specific phrase describing your own high school experience. Rewrite the paragraph, adding details that help the reader visualize the high school you attended and what you did there. Replace vague words and statements with specific ones from your own life.

### Undeveloped Paragraph

High school for me was quite an experience. I still remember many of the classes I took and some of the teachers. There were many social events, and I participated in several extracurricular activities. All of this affected me, and I changed in a number of ways during my high school years.

## Challenge Exercise: Paragraph Development

The following paragraph is too short; it stays on the topic but lacks development. Rewrite the paragraph, expanding on the statements by elaborating on the ideas expressed and including examples. Replace vague words with specific ones that will better explain the effects of the fiscal crisis of 2008.

## Undeveloped Paragraph

The fiscal crisis had a big impact on the United States. It changed people's attitudes toward the government and politics. It also changed the way they felt about jobs and careers. It made them think differently about credit cards, saving money, investing, and buying property.

WRITING ASSIGNMENT: Basic, Intermediate, Challenge

## Basic Writing Assignment: Paragraph Development

Choose a topic from the list that follows. Before composing your paragraph, do whatever kind of prewriting activity works best for you—focused writing, brainstorming, clustering, and so on. Look over your prewriting and find a sentence that states a significant idea about the topic. Begin the paragraph with this statement as your topic sentence. Be sure to include plenty of supporting details.

1. A job you enjoyed
2. A surprising event
3. Your experience with credit cards
4. Your biggest accomplishment
5. A problematic relationship
6. An older person you admire
7. Your experience with Facebook

## Intermediate Writing Assignment: Paragraph Development

Choose a topic from the list that follows. Before composing your paragraph, do whatever kind of prewriting activity works best for you—focused writing, brainstorming, clustering, and so on.

Look over your prewriting and find a sentence that states a significant idea about the topic. Begin the paragraph with this statement as your topic sentence. Be sure to include plenty of supporting details.

1. How to solve a problem in your neighborhood
2. How to solve a problem at your college
3. Your attitude toward smoking
4. What you will major in and why
5. Why you like or dislike reality television
6. Your attitude toward advertising
7. Why you do or do not vote

## Challenge Writing Assignment: Paragraph Development

Choose a topic from the list that follows. Before composing your paragraph, do whatever kind of prewriting activity works best for you—focused writing, brainstorming, clustering, and so on. Look over your prewriting and find a sentence that states a significant idea about the topic. Begin the paragraph with this statement as your topic sentence. Be sure to include plenty of supporting details.

1. What we should do about immigration
2. Why we should study history
3. Why medical costs have risen so rapidly
4. How technology affects the classroom
5. Why we should read book reviews or film reviews
6. What the term *ethnic studies* means today
7. Where technology will take us in ten years

# Coherence

Sentences in a paragraph should be arranged in a clear, logical order. **Coherence** means that all the parts of something *cohere*, or hang together. To make a computer, you must have all the right parts, but you also have to fit them together correctly so the computer will work. To write a coherent paragraph, make every sentence follow from the one before. The sentences should flow naturally, like numbers in a row—1, 2, 3, 4, 5. They should not jump around without any pattern like random numbers—3, 8, 1, 7, 2, 5.

Here is a paragraph that lacks coherence.

*The plot of the film is full of surprises. It is about two women, one a clone of the other. The woman gets in trouble after she discovers that her boyfriend is mixed up with a drug cartel. Her boyfriend finds out about her illness and plans to dump her for the healthy clone. The drug gang ends up killing her clone by accident when their car bomb goes off with her hiding in the car. But first the drug gang that is chasing her boyfriend kidnaps her clone, who is pretending to be her, and tries to find out where her boyfriend is. The boyfriend gets into a wild shootout with the gang but survives. She has a terminal disease so she agrees to have herself cloned by a new process that will make a healthy copy of her. The final surprise is that the original woman decides to pretend she is the clone and not tell her boyfriend. He turns out to be part of another gang that has surrounded the kidnappers. The heroine's boyfriend thinks that she is dead and her clone is the one who is still alive and decides to marry her. The woman herself is an ordinary, law-abiding person working in a television newsroom.*

Although the first sentence in the preceding paragraph is a clear and specific topic sentence and all of the following statements support it, it is impossible to follow the plot. Obviously something more than a topic sentence and unity is needed: the paragraph has to be coherent. Here is the same paragraph arranged in a coherent order.

*The plot of the film is full of surprises. It is about two women, one a clone of the other. The woman herself is an ordinary, law-abiding person working in a television newsroom. She has a terminal disease so she agrees to have herself cloned by a new process that will make a healthy copy of her. The woman gets in trouble after she discovers that her boyfriend is mixed up with a drug cartel. Her boyfriend finds out about her illness and plans to dump her for the healthy clone. But first the drug gang that is chasing her boyfriend kidnaps her clone, who is pretending to be her, and tries to find out where her boyfriend is. The drug gang ends up killing her clone by accident when their car bomb goes off with her hiding in the car. The boyfriend gets into a wild shootout with the gang but survives. He turns out to be part of another gang that has surrounded the kidnappers. The heroine's boyfriend thinks that she is dead and her clone is the one who is still alive and decides to marry her. The final surprise is that the original woman decides to pretend she is the clone and not tell her boyfriend.*

## Transitions

Coherent paragraphs move the reader along smoothly from beginning to end. To make the connections clearer to the reader, use **transitional expressions.** Transitional expressions are like road signs to help your readers see where you are taking them.

## Transitional Words and Phrases

Here is a list of the most frequently used transitional words and phrases. Remember to use them sometimes (but not too often!) in your paragraphs.

| | |
|---|---|
| **For Adding Information** | also, and, besides, first (second, third), furthermore, in addition, likewise, moreover, too |
| **For Showing Opposites and Contrast** | although, but, even though, however, nevertheless, on the other hand, still, yet |
| **For Showing Time** | after, afterward, at last, at that time, before, during, earlier, later, meanwhile, since, soon, then, while |
| **For Showing Place** | above, adjacent to, behind, below, beyond, farther, here, nearby, next to, opposite to, to the left, to the right |
| **For Showing Results or Conclusions** | as a result, consequently, finally, hence, in conclusion, so, then, therefore, thus |
| **For Showing Examples** | chiefly, especially, for example, for instance, for one thing, namely, particularly, specifically |

---

### EXERCISES USING TRANSITIONAL EXPRESSIONS:
Basic, Intermediate, Challenge

**Please note:** If you have difficulty with sentence grammar while doing these exercises, you may want to look ahead to Chapter 7 for explanations of sentence fragments, comma splices, and run-on sentences.

## Basic Exercise: Transitional Expressions

Use words from this list to make transitions in the sentences below. Be sure to use logically correct words, and watch your punctuation!

| | |
|---|---|
| and | moreover |
| besides | nevertheless |
| but | on the other hand |
| consequently | soon |
| however | therefore |
| meanwhile | then |

1. Alexis likes to read novels, _____ she does not like to write essays about them.
2. Josh was on the phone for an hour with Jessica; _____ Vanessa was trying to call him.
3. The party was already over; _____, everyone was tired and wanted to go home.
4. The sign indicated a delay ahead; _____ James took the next turnoff.
5. The pay was good, _____ the work was interesting.
6. They kept spending money on lottery tickets; _____ they didn't have enough left to pay the rent.
7. We waited for a while at the corner; _____ we decided to look for them elsewhere.

## Intermediate Exercise: Transitional Expressions

Connect each pair of sentences using correct punctuation and one of the following transitional expressions. Be sure that the transition is logical.

| | |
|---|---|
| afterward | for example |
| although | however |
| as well as | in addition |
| at last | in fact |
| especially | therefore |

1. There are numerous ways to prevent plagiarism. The committee has proposed seven.
2. The scenery and costumes were finished. The actors were well rehearsed and impatient to begin.
3. Several states had budget shortfalls. New York and California had deficits in the billions of dollars.

4. Security at airports has been tightened. Such measures alone will not prevent terrorism.
5. The hikers wandered for miles through the forest. They came to a highway.
6. The site has not been zoned for business. The town will have to plan residential developments there.
7. The friends had dinner at a restaurant near the campus. They went to a club in town.

## Challenge Exercise: Transitional Expressions

In the following paragraph, some transitional words are missing. In each blank, write the correct transitional expression from the list below.

| | |
|---|---|
| although | then |
| at last | therefore |
| however | while |
| in addition | |

The influences that Gabriel José García Márquez, _____ he now lives in Mexico City, owes much of his character as a writer to his experiences as a child in Colombia, the land of his birth. He spent his early childhood in the town of Aracataca, where a strike by banana workers around the time of his birth in 1928 was ended by the army shooting many workers. This event, _____ to the following years of political violence, found its way into the stories he heard as a child. In his early years he was raised mostly by his grandparents because his parents were struggling financially. His grandfather died when he was eight, and his grandmother began to go blind. _____ he returned to the care of his parents, who sent him to an elementary school called the Cartagena de Indias School in Barranquilla. _____ he was there, he impressed the teachers with the extent of his reading. _____ his father attempted to set up a pharmacy in the town of Sucre and took his family there. _____, since there was no adequate secondary school there, his parents sent him to a Jesuit school called Colegio San José de la Compañía de Jesús in Barranquilla. At that school he achieved recognition for his ability to recite long passages of poetry and to write satires, which he called "dumb things of mine." _____ he was on his way to becoming a writer.

—Information from Gabriel José García Márquez, *Living to Tell the Tale*, trans. Edith Grossman (New York: Knopf, 2003).

# Sequence

To be coherent, a paragraph has to be arranged in a certain order. Different kinds of paragraphs are arranged differently—according to chronological sequence, spatial sequence, or climactic sequence.

## Chronological Sequence

Probably the simplest and easiest method of organizing a paragraph is to tell a series of events or facts in the order they occurred. Time order, or **chronological sequence,** is the method of development used in **narrative** writing, such as fiction, history, or biography. Paragraphs in time sequence are easier to follow if you use transitional expressions or **time markers** that signal location in time, such as *first, next, before, after, soon, at last, when, while,* and *then.* Such connections give the reader a clear sense of unfolding events. You should also use specific time references whenever they are appropriate, such as *the next day, the following week,* or *a year later.*

### Sample Paragraph in Chronological Sequence

Read the paragraph below and notice how the writer uses chronological sequence. Find the transitional expressions and time markers that help to hold the paragraph together.

> *Jeffrey wanted to buy a laptop computer or a netbook for his trip to the Caribbean, so he decided to use a systematic approach. First he asked three of his friends what kinds of computers they owned, what they paid for them, and how well they liked them. Each one had a different answer, but they all liked the ones they had. One had an Apple Ipad and insisted that it was better than any laptop or netbook. Another had a large laptop computer, which she liked best but found too large to use while traveling. The third had a very light netbook, which he insisted was the best to use on a trip. Next, since Jeffrey's friends disagreed, he went to a small electronics store in his neighborhood, where the clerk tried to sell him one of the two high-priced netbooks they had available. Ronald was still not satisfied and went to a much larger store that sold all kinds of high-tech equipment. Here he was able to look at many makes, compare prices, and*

*discuss the pros and cons of Ipads and netbooks with a well-informed*
*clerk. At this point, he was beginning to feel more knowledgeable but*
*not yet ready to make a purchase. Finally, he searched the Web for*
*information on netbooks and Ipads, read some evaluations and com-*
*plaints by consumers, and found a discount site where he was able*
*to buy a netbook he had seen in the store, but for ten percent less. He*
*felt satisfied that he had made the right choice.*

## Spatial Sequence

Another way of achieving coherence in your paragraphs is by arranging statements in **spatial sequence.** This means that your description
follows the placement of items in space, for example, inside to outside, front to back, side to side, up to down, near to far. As with time
sequence, be sure not to leave any confusing gaps, and use enough
details so that the reader has a clear picture of what you are describing. The paragraph should guide the reader's gaze in some recogniz-
able direction or pattern, like a camera panning over a scene, using
**spatial markers,** such as *above, below, to the right, to the left, ahead,*
and *behind.*

### Sample Paragraph in Spatial Sequence

Read the paragraph below and notice how the writer uses spatial
sequence. Find the transitional expressions and location markers
that help to hold the paragraph together.

*After observing the front of the building, visitors were always sur-*
*prised when they went inside. Its exterior lent it the appearance of a*
*classical government structure of the early twentieth century, with*
*a prominent overhang like that of a Greek temple looming above*
*the entrance, supported below by a row of Corinthian columns. At*
*the street level, but slightly to the right of center, stood the impos-*
*ing double doors with their elaborate oak carvings. Once within*
*the gleaming entrance hall, however, visitors suddenly blinked at the*
*halogen lighting, the steel and leather furniture on both sides, the*
*large potted plants in the corners, and abstract paintings brightening*
*the walls. Straight ahead, a bank of polished escalators ran smoothly*

*up to an atrium lit from above by sunlight streaming through a glass ceiling. The effect was that of a totally new building constructed behind a traditional facade.*

## Climactic Sequence

A third kind of paragraph arrangement is called **climactic sequence**. In this arrangement, sentences build to a climax. They start with less important or less emphatic statements and end with the most important or most emphatic statements. Climactic sequence is useful in developing **expository** or **persuasive** paragraphs that discuss ideas rather than tell stories or describe places. A paragraph in climactic sequence may give a series of facts, reasons, or examples to support a point. When you write such paragraphs, be sure to include enough facts and ideas to support your point, and make each sentence develop logically from the one before. Use transitional expressions such as *moreover, however, furthermore, therefore, in addition, consequently,* and *in conclusion.* Include **relational markers** as well, such as *more convincing, equally important, more important, just as significant, worth considering,* and *above all.*

### Sample Paragraph in Climactic Sequence

Read the paragraph below and notice how the writer uses climactic sequence. Find the transitional expressions and relational markers that help to hold the paragraph together.

*Learning a second language requires effort and persistence, but it brings many benefits. First, as form of mental exercise it sharpens your memory and helps you think more clearly. It also teaches you the structure of grammar, including the parts of speech and the way they work in your own language. Just as significantly, it can make traveling more interesting because you can understand a country better when you speak the language. In today's global economy, where business is conducted in many languages, being able to speak a second language can make you more employable as well. Even more important, knowing a second language allows you to appreciate great works of literature and films in their original languages in a way that people who have to rely on translations cannot. Above all, learning a second language means acquiring another culture, which makes you a richer, more aware, more open-minded, and finer human being.*

## Key Words from Chapter 3 for Review

chronological sequence, climactic sequence, coherence, expository, narrative, paragraph development, persuasive, relational markers, spatial markers, spatial sequence, time markers, transitional expressions

CHAPTER

# Creating Varied Paragraphs

---

## STEPPING UP: WRITING TIP 4

You should learn to write many types of paragraphs effectively. So that you can acquire the skills needed to develop your paragraphs in various ways, we will look at the different kinds of paragraphs as if they always existed in pure form. In more advanced writing, you may find that the different categories are sometimes mixed, especially within whole essays. You will practice writing paragraphs in each of the different modes (descriptive, narrative, expository, and persuasive) so that later you will have the skills to compose whole essays using strategies suited to any mode you might choose.

---

## Types of Paragraphs

Different kinds of writing require different kinds of paragraphs. The four chief categories of writing—narration, description, exposition, and persuasion—are often called the **rhetorical modes.**

- If the purpose of a paragraph is to tell about an event, we call it a **narrative.** It will generally be organized in **chronological sequence.**
- If its purpose is to create an impression of a person, place, or object, we call it **descriptive.** It will likely be arranged in

**spatial sequence,** moving from one location to another, although there may sometimes be some narration included.

- If it is meant to help us understand something, we call it **expository.** (Expository writing includes comparison, process analysis, definition, classification, and cause/effect analysis.) Expository essays most often use **climactic sequence** but they can also include elements of narration or description.

- A paragraph that tries to convince us of something is called **persuasive.** It will probably be in climactic sequence so that it builds up to the most convincing points near the end, although it too may contain elements of other modes.

Few larger pieces of writing fit totally into these rhetorical modes, but most belong primarily in one mode while making use of others. By creating paragraphs in separate modes, you will be better able to compose whole essays, business reports, research papers, and creative works. Composing paragraphs in separate modes is like practicing separate skills in a sport: You can work on your three-point shots, slam dunks, free throws, and defense separately during practice, but when you play the game, you must use them all at the right time.

## Narration: Telling About an Event

Telling about experiences that happened to you or other people is called **narrative writing.**\* Many short stories, novels, and history books are in this form. In narrative writing, paragraphs tell parts of a larger story and are written in **time sequence.** A narrative paragraph should (1) have enough details to give the reader a close-up of the events, (2) contain **transitional expressions,** especially **time markers,** to help the reader follow the sequence of actions, and (3) be written in one verb tense, usually the **past tense,** since the paragraph is usually about actions that happened in the past.

Narrative writing can be done in either the first person or the third person. In the first person, you are writing about something you experienced yourself, using *I* and *me* frequently in telling the story. In the third person, you are telling about something another person or persons did, using *he* or *she* frequently, if it happened to only one person, and *they* if it happened to more than one.

---

\*Note: If you have difficulties with grammar, it may help to study Chapter 9, especially "Recognizing Verb Tenses," while working on narration.

### Sample Paragraph: Narrative, First Person

Read the paragraph below, paying attention to the way the student who wrote it stays in the first person, using *I* and *me* to tell the entire story from her own point of view.

> *First impressions can really be misleading. Last October I met "Dominic," who gave me the impression he was interested in an authentic relationship with me. My cousin, who was in the same computer class as he was, thought he was the sort of guy I would like. He had a sense of humor, a lot of intelligence, and a full-time job. We went out a few times to clubs and saw a film together. I was really getting interested in him when he asked me out to an expensive restaurant to try the food from his country. I thought he was even more interesting because he liked to talk about how they did things in "my country," as he called it. He had a lot of traditional attitudes and ways of doing things, and mainly he was a gentleman. Even though we disagreed about the role of women in society, we got along really well. I thought our restaurant date was supposed to be a chance to talk about getting really serious about each other. Little did I know it was just a way of letting me know what was really going on. The next day he called me and said he had to go back to his country because his parents had arranged for him to get married in two months to a woman they had chosen for him. He thanked me for all the companionship and said we would always be friends. Needless to say, I was too stunned to be angry. Later my cousin said she thought he just invented the marriage story as an excuse for breaking up, but I think he was sincere and maybe didn't really mean to let things get so serious. Next time I'll know better.*

In telling about your own experiences, use the **first person** (*I*, *we*) as in the paragraph above. In telling about an event that happened to someone else, use the **third person** (*she, he, it, they*). When you start a paragraph in the first person, stay in the first person; when you start in the third person, stay in the third person. Choose one specific event and stick to it. The sample paragraph that follows is written in the third person.

## Sample Paragraph: Narrative, Third Person

Read the paragraph below, paying attention to the way the entire paragraph uses *she*, *her*, and the author's name to tell the story of a famous author's life in the third person.

*The life of novelist Amy Tan can be summed up in one word—unpredictable. Although her hard work and ultimate success may seem typical of immigrant families, her path to fame took many surprising turns. Her mother and father, both immigrants who had escaped the Communist takeover of China in 1949, raised Amy and her two brothers in northern California. When Amy was in high school, however, her father and oldest brother both died of brain tumors within a single year. Soon afterward, Amy's mother took her and her brother to Switzerland. But Amy and her mother did not get along, and when her mother sent her to a Baptist college, Amy chose instead to go with her boyfriend to San Jose City College. Next, Amy rejected her mother's ambitions for her by dropping out of her pre-med major and earning a B.A. and M.A. in English and linguistics. After she and her boyfriend married, she tried a Ph.D. program but dropped out and worked for a while in helping the developmentally disabled. Then she and a partner set up a speech writing company until the two had a dispute and Amy became a freelance business writer. Soon, needing more creativity, she tried jazz piano and, at last, fiction writing. Once her early stories began to be published, a literary agent recognized her talent, and she was on the way to writing The Joy Luck Club and her other well-known novels. In 2003 she published an autobiography in which she told about how she suffered severe symptoms of Lyme disease, which caused her to stop writing temporarily. Since then she has started writing again but spends some of her time helping to raise awareness of Lyme disease.*

—From "Amy Tan: Best-Selling Novelist," Academy of Achievement. September 3, 2007; www.achievement.org/autodoc/page/tan0bio-1. Revised June 17, 2010.

---

WRITING ASSIGNMENT: Basic, Intermediate, Challenge

## Basic Writing Assignment: Narrative Paragraphs

Write a narrative paragraph in the first person on one of the topics below. Do focused writing on the topic to create a rough draft. Then look over the draft and check to see if you have begun with a sentence that points the reader in a clear direction. Check whether you have developed the story in enough detail for the reader to visualize it. Add more details and transitional expressions, especially time markers, as needed. Write a final draft.

1. Having an unexpected experience in a classroom
2. Having a problem with your car
3. Coming down with an illness
4. Visiting a place you haven't seen in a long time
5. Acting on bad advice
6. Meeting a famous person
7. Enjoying a celebration

## Intermediate Writing Assignment: Narrative Paragraphs

Write a narrative paragraph in the first person on one of the topics below. While telling what happened, try also to explain the meaning of the story. Do focused writing on the topic to create a rough draft. Then look over the draft and check to see if you have begun with a sentence that points the reader in a clear direction. Check whether you have developed the story in enough detail for the reader to visualize it. Add more details and transitional words, especially time markers, as needed. Write a final draft.

1. Identifying your own strengths by applying to college and being accepted
2. Learning from your relationship with a disabled person
3. Realizing your true self through facing and resolving a conflict
4. Understanding yourself better through winning a competition
5. Being misunderstood by a group and learning from it
6. Confronting a truth about yourself through an experience of fear
7. Becoming more mature through an experience of loss

## Challenge Writing Assignment: Narrative Paragraphs

Write a narrative paragraph in the third person on one of the topics to follow. Do focused writing on the topic to create a rough draft. Then look over the draft and check to see if you have begun with a sentence that points the reader in a clear direction. Check whether you have developed the story in enough detail for the reader to visualize it. If necessary, do some research to find out enough facts to develop your paragraph well. Add more details and transitional words, especially time markers, as needed. Write a final draft.

1. Write a paragraph summarizing a film you have seen.
2. Write a paragraph summarizing a story you have read.
3. Write a paragraph summarizing a news story in the headlines.
4. Write a paragraph telling about how your family moved from one city or country to another.
5. Write a one-paragraph account of a sporting event you witnessed.
6. Write a paragraph explaining how someone you know changed as he or she grew up.
7. Write a paragraph telling how a situation in your college or your neighborhood has gotten better or worse.

# Description: Visualizing Persons, Places, and Objects

Descriptive writing conveys an impression to the reader by appealing to the five senses. An effective description gives a unified impression in which all the details contribute to the same overall feeling about the person, place, or object. Usually, descriptive paragraphs follow a spatial pattern of organization, moving from one place to another, from top to bottom, from inside to outside, or from near to far. Descriptive effects are also frequently part of narrative and expository writing as well. To write a vivid, unified description, limit your subject so that you can give a full, distinct picture of it.

WRITING EXERCISES: Basic, Intermediate, Challenge

## Basic Exercise: Descriptive Paragraphs

The paragraph below describes a person. To help the reader visualize the person, supply a key word in the topic sentence at the beginning and descriptive words in the other blanks. Try to use distinctive, powerful words that appeal to the senses, and avoid using too many vague words. Name the predominant impression that the paragraph creates, and identify which of the five senses are appealed to in your description.

Grace is a really _____ person. She has a _____ personality and a _____ appearance. Her _____ manner and _____ face always make other people feel _____. Because of her _____ way of talking, she creates an unforgettable impression. All of these qualities cause people to remember her after only meeting her once.

## Intermediate Exercise: Descriptive Paragraphs

The paragraph below describes a room. Write a key word in the first sentence to give an overall impression, and supply descriptive words in the blanks so that the reader can visualize the room. Try to appeal to the five senses in your choice of words, and give preference to specific, vivid modifiers over vague words. Tell what kind of spatial sequence is used.

Overall, the house looked _____. The living room was decorated with _____ wallpaper and had a _____ carpet. The furniture appeared _____ and created a _____ impression. Then, when one walked into the _____ dining room, one saw _____ cabinets and _____ appliances. Down a _____ hallway, one reached two bedrooms, one of which was decorated in a _____ style, making it feel _____. The other, by contrast, was obviously more _____ because of the _____ and _____ located against the walls. This was definitely a _____ house.

## Challenge Exercise: Descriptive Paragraphs

Complete the paragraph below so that it describes a neighborhood in such a way that a reader can achieve a three-dimensional, sensory impression of it. Begin with a key word in the first sentence to hold the description together, and supply descriptive words where needed. As always, be specific in your choices.

As Andrew opened the book for the first time, he could tell that it was a _____ novel. It was set in a _____ neighborhood, which had a _____ atmosphere. The main character was a _____ young woman, who gave the impression that she had a very _____ personality and a _____ mind. As the story began, she was walking along the aisles of a _____ grocery, looking with a _____ glance at all the _____ goods lined up on the _____ shelves. She seemed to be lost in her own thoughts, when suddenly a _____ man approached her with a _____ look on his _____ face.

---

WRITING ASSIGNMENT: Basic, Intermediate, Challenge

## Basic Writing Assignment: Details in Descriptive Paragraphs

Write a paragraph describing yourself. Begin with a topic sentence containing a key word that will hold the paragraph together: "I am a _____ person." Do some brainstorming once you have chosen this key word, writing down all the details you can think of about yourself that illustrate this quality. Write an exploratory draft; then look it over to see what descriptive words can be replaced with more specific, vivid ones.

## Intermediate Writing Assignment: Spatial Sequence in Descriptive Paragraphs

Think of a place that is familiar to you, such as a bus or train station, a courtroom, a classroom, a shopping mall, a church, mosque, or synagogue, a supermarket, or a computer café. Visualize the scene as specifically as you can, and brainstorm all the descriptive details you can remember. Arrange the items in two or three spatial categories, such as front, middle, back, or left, middle, right. Then write an exploratory draft, remembering to begin with a topic sentence in which a key word or phrase identifies the overall quality of the place. Read over your draft to find gaps that need transitional expressions. Make any improvements in word choice or grammar that are needed. Write a final draft.

## Challenge Writing Assignment: Descriptive Paragraphs

Think of a well-known person whom you especially like or dislike. Find a key word that you think sums up that person's attractive or unattractive qualities. Write a topic sentence. Then brainstorm or do some focused writing to explore all the details that can be used to illustrate that quality of the person. Find details that reveal something about the person's character and style, not just his or her appearance. Write a paragraph describing that person. Read your draft, noticing whether you have chosen specific descriptive words and transitional expressions. Write a revised draft.

## Comparison: Exploring Similarities and Differences

Creating paragraphs that compare people, places, experiences, or concepts is a valuable kind of writing practice. It will strengthen your ability to develop and analyze topics. Although few essays are devoted entirely to **comparison**, an experienced writer should be able to make clear, thoughtful comparisons whenever necessary.

When you compare, be sure to discuss both subjects together. Begin your paragraph with a topic sentence that mentions *both* persons or things. This way you will avoid the trap of discussing first one and then the other, leaving the reader to figure out how the subjects are similar or different. Which of these two sentences makes a better beginning for a comparison?

1. Earning a General Equivalency Diploma is easier than graduating from high school.
2. Thomas studied hard to earn his General Equivalency Diploma.

Either sentence might make a good topic sentence for a paragraph, but only Sentence 1 starts off with a comparison. We expect the writer to prove that it takes more work, time, and study to finish high school than it does to prepare for the GED.

### Three Kinds of Comparison

| | |
|---|---|
| **Parallels:** | Pointing out similarities between two people or things |
| **Contrasts:** | Pointing out differences between two people or things |
| **Comparison/Contrast:** | Pointing out both similarities and differences between two people or things |

The following three paragraphs illustrate the three main kinds of comparison. The first discusses the similarities between two countries, the second contrasts the differences between two sisters, and the third explores both the similarities and the differences between two jobs a student held. Notice that the topic sentences are focused and that they all make comparative statements.

## Paragraph 1: Two Similar Subjects

*As island monarchies, Japan and Great Britain have much in common. Both are small in land area but heavily populated, and both used to rely on the sea for food, imports, and export trade. Both have huge capital cities that have played major roles in world affairs, and both have been in the forefront of industrial development. Although the surrounding ocean has enabled both to remain culturally isolated during some periods in history, the nearness of continental powers has been the source of many wars for both countries over the centuries. Both peoples, in fact, derive from their neighboring continents, and their languages have close ties to continental languages—Japanese to Chinese picture-writing and English to German and French. Over the centuries both nations have presided over great empires, both of which have disintegrated.*

## Paragraph 2: Two Contrasting Subjects

*My two sisters are so different in their attitude toward work that it is hard to believe they come from the same family. Jill has always been a workaholic, while Joy always wanted to have a good time. When they were little girls, Joy would be skinning her knees in rollerblade races and begging Dad for money to buy candy, while Jill was earning Mom's approval for her help with cooking and cleaning. In school Jill studied diligently and brought home stacks of homework. Joy, on the other hand, discovered that school was a social whirl and considered high grades the sign of a boring personality. In high school, when Joy was the favorite cheerleader, Jill was president of the honor society. Although Joy dropped out of college after two months, she has joined a country music group and expects to have a career on television without needing any higher education. Jill, with an M.B.A. and piles of honors, is making her way up the corporate ladder.*

## Paragraph 3: Two Subjects That Are Partly Similar and Partly Different

*Baxter had two jobs that required some of the same skills but offered different rewards. As both coach of a lacrosse team and as Web site manager for a company that arranged tours to Central and*

*South America, he had to understand people. He had to empathize with and motivate his players, especially when the team was losing. As a Webmaster, he had to understand what would motivate customers to buy his company's service. Both jobs demanded good judgment and enough creativity to produce results, and both jobs gave him experience that he could use in his career. Despite these similarities, the satisfaction from the two jobs was different. The Webmaster job paid well and allowed him to feel independent, but it left him feeling detached from people. Coaching, on the other hand, gave him the satisfaction of inspiring teamwork and helping a whole group of kids grow together, but it did not pay well enough for him to remain in the job. In the future, he hopes to find a career where he can use all of his skills and have the benefits of both jobs.*

## Attention to Detail

One important skill necessary in making good comparisons is the ability to notice many detailed similarities and differences. When beginning writers do not succeed in their efforts to compare, they often have not done enough brainstorming. They have found only a few similarities or differences and then given up. For practice, let's consider the similarities and differences, discovered by a student named Steve, between being in the army and working in an accounting firm. After energetic brainstorming, Steve thought of many similarities and differences.

Steve's Experience of Serving in the Army vs. Working in an Accounting Firm

| Similarities | Differences |
| --- | --- |
| hard work in both | outdoor work in army; all indoors in firm |
| both required special training | hard basic training in army; short orientation period but learn on the job in accounting firm |
| worked mostly with men but with some women in both . | military training tried to "make us men"; no emphasis on gender in company |
| had living quarters provided | lived in army barracks; lived at home when working |
| continued to learn in both situations | received electronics training in military; took night courses while working in firm |

| discipline needed in both | discipline imposed by officers in army; needed self-discipline to complete tasks in accounting physical and mental discipline in army; only mental discipline in accounting job |
| both provided upward opportunities | army would have required reenlisting; accounting requires further degrees, which is my goal |
| dress code in both stayed in both about two years | uniform in military; conservative jacket and tie in business office assigned to many places in military; worked in same office in accounting firm |
| liked both experiences | hated military at first but got to like it; liked accounting job but started to get bored and wanted to move up |

WRITING EXERCISES: Basic, Intermediate, Challenge

## Basic Exercise: Comparative Paragraphs

Practice making comparative statements. Fill in the blanks with correct comparative words or phrases. Try to use precise, specific words rather than vague ones. You may want to review the use of modifiers on page 197.

1. Stephanie is _____ than Carol.
2. Our team played _____ than theirs.
3. I bought this car because it is _____ than the other one.
4. Stanley's PDA is just as _____ as Karen's.
5. Hector's apartment is just as _____ as Jeremy's.
6. Emily's video is _____ than anything we've seen on YouTube.
7. Bradley was drafted for the team because he _____ than the rest of the players on the list.

## Intermediate Exercise: Comparative Paragraphs

Complete these sentences by comparing each subject with a comparable one. Try to use precise, specific comparative phrases that might serve as key words for paragraphs.

1. The film I saw yesterday was _____.
2. My biology professor is _____.

3. The food in this restaurant is _____.
4. That news anchor is _____.
5. This poem contains _____.
6. My last vacation was _____.
7. My grades this semester were _____.

## Challenge Exercise: Comparative Paragraphs

Create comparative sentences using the two persons, groups, or things in each pair. Try to use precise, specific comparative phrases that might serve as key words for paragraphs.

1. owning a car vs. using public transportation
2. student newspapers vs. commercial newspapers
3. attending college full time vs. working while attending part time
4. homeschooling vs. public schools
5. seeing a movie on a DVD at home vs. seeing it in a theater
6. reading a book about an event vs. seeing a documentary on it
7. lecture classes vs. discussion classes

WRITING ASSIGNMENT: Basic, Intermediate, Challenge

## Basic Writing Assignment: Comparative Paragraphs

Brainstorm and make a list of all the similarities between yourself and another person close to you, such as a sibling, cousin, or friend. Write an exploratory draft beginning with a comparative topic sentence such as "My sister and I are both ambitious people" or "My brother and I have identical tastes." Look over your work and read it aloud to someone else. Decide what needs to be added, changed, or deleted. Be sure to use **comparative markers** showing similarity, such as *both, as . . . as, neither, like, alike, the same, in the same way, equal,* and *similar.* Revise and write a final draft.

## Intermediate Writing Assignment: Comparative Paragraphs

Do some brainstorming or focused writing on the differences between two jobs you have had or two schools you have attended. Make a list of the differences. Then create a comparative statement for your topic sentence that provides a map for the paragraph, such as "I learned more on Job A than on Job B" or "College X was more academically rigorous than College Y." Finally, compose a paragraph comparing the two. Look over your work and read it aloud to someone else. Decide what needs to be added, changed, or deleted. Be sure to use comparative markers showing differences, such as *more, more than, less, less than, better, worse, by contrast, on the other hand, different, differently,* and *however.* Revise and write a final draft.

## Challenge Writing Assignment: Comparative Paragraphs

Write a paragraph in which you point out both similarities and differences between two famous people. Brainstorm and make a list of the differences and similarities between two people in the news, one you like better than the other. Choose two persons in the same general category, such as entertainers, political figures, or religious leaders. Make two lists: on the left side list all the similarities between them, and on the right list the differences. Write an exploratory draft beginning with a comparative topic sentence such as "Steve Martin and Tyler Perry are both hilarious slapstick comedians, but their styles are different." Look over your work and read it aloud to someone else. Decide what needs to be added, changed, or deleted. Be sure to use comparative markers showing similarity, such as *both, as . . . as, neither, like, alike, the same, in the same way, equal,* and *similar.* Also use words showing difference, such as *more, more than, less, less than, better, worse, by contrast, on the other hand, different, differently,* and *however.* Revise and write a final draft.

# Exposition: "How-to" and Process Paragraphs

Explaining how something develops is called **process analysis.** Explaining how to do something on the job is called **procedural writing.** Paragraphs of this kind follow a step-by-step sequence, and are usually not difficult to organize. However, they do demand great care: You have to be unusually clear and thorough because you cannot use hand gestures, point directions with your finger, or ask questions to see if your listener understands the way we do when speaking aloud.

You also have to make sure that the reader can understand all of your terms. If you are writing for experts, use specialized terms; if you are writing for general readers, use no more technical vocabulary than necessary and explain the meaning of all technical terms you do use.

## Basic Exercise: How-to Paragraphs

"How-to" paragraphs should be held together by transitional words that refer to steps in a sequence, such as *first, next, then, after,* and *finally.* Underline the transitional words in this paragraph.

Doing your best on an essay assignment requires a systematic method. Before you do any writing, read the instructions and topics carefully so that you understand all of the possible topics. If there are any that are not clear to you, be sure to ask the professor for clarification to help you make your choice. Next, select your topic according to your preparation and knowledge. Then, preparatory to actually writing, jot down the main parts of the essay and some of the important facts to support each main point. Do some brainstorming or other kind of freewriting to get a feel for the topic. Only at this point are you ready to write. When you begin to compose, be sure that your introductory paragraph includes a plan or "map" for your whole essay so that you and the grader will know just what you intend to cover. At last it is time to write the main body paragraphs and show how much you know about the subject. Be sure to include plenty of facts. If possible, end with a concluding paragraph that restates your chief ideas without repeating the words of the introduction. Finally, read your paper twice: once for errors in spelling, grammar, and phrasing, and once for revisions of content. If you have done all this, you may earn an A, but even if you don't, you can feel confident that you have done your best.

## Intermediate Exercise: How-to Paragraphs

The following paragraph is about how cellular phones work. Is it written for laypersons (nonspecialists) or for experts? Identify the technical terms in this paragraph.

Cell phones work almost like two-way radios. But compared to the old walkie-talkies and CB radios, cell phones have enormous geographical range. Every city has many cells of about ten square miles each; every cell has a base station with a transmitting tower. Cell phones transmit on two frequencies between the cell phone and the base station; that way, unlike CB radios, both people can talk at the same time. Every carrier within a given city also has an MTSO (Mobile Telephone Switching Office) which supervises all calls through the base stations. When someone receives a call, the MTSO locates the phone by using a control channel and sets up a pair of frequencies for the callers to use. If a caller is moving toward the edge of his or her cell, the base station in that cell notices that the signal is weakening and coordinates through the MTSO with the next cell base station. As the person begins to leave one cell, the signal is switched to the next base station. If the cell phone's SID (System Identification Code) is not within the control channel of the cell the person is in, the nearby MTSO communicates with the MTSO of the person's home system to make sure the SID is valid. Then the local MTSO tracks the call. This is called roaming, a system which allows even greater geographical range in cell phone communication. All of these contacts are nearly instantaneous.

—Marshall Brain, Jeff Tyson, and Julia Layton, "How Cell Phones Work," *How Stuff Works*, 2011; www.electronics.howstuffworks.com/cell-phone.htm.

## Challenge Exercise: Process Paragraphs

Here is a paragraph explaining a developmental process. This one is about how a particular neurological disorder develops. Count the number of stages mentioned in the paragraph, and identify transitional words and time markers.

Attention-deficit hyperactivity disorder (ADHD), a condition affecting many students at all levels of education, probably begins at birth but usually is not recognized until later. In the preschool years, children with ADHD demonstrate symptoms such as impatience with waiting in line, staying in a seat, or completing a task. Since nearly all children behave this way at times, children with ADHD are often not identified right away. Once in school, such students are more likely to be identified by their tendency to perform erratically, jumping from one project to another and failing to meet deadlines. The best schools today have the means at this stage of children's development to give these students psychological and neurological tests. If satisfactory evaluations are made, ADHD students then receive special learning tools, coaching, and family support to help them succeed academically. As they become young adults, persons with ADHD who do not have such support may continue to become easily distracted, lose important objects needed for completion of work assignments, and have difficulty organizing tasks and sustaining focus. They may, however, benefit from medications such as mood stabilizers and beta blockers, which can alleviate some of these symptoms.

—From *Professional Guide to Diseases,* 5th Ed. (Springhouse, Pennsylvania: Springhouse Corporation, 1995), 409–11.

WRITING ASSIGNMENT: Basic, Intermediate, Challenge

## Basic Writing Assignment: How-to Paragraphs

Write a paragraph explaining exactly how to get from your home to another location, such as the place where you work or your college classroom. Imagine that the person reading it will not be able to talk with you or ask questions if he or she gets mixed up but will have to depend entirely on your instructions to find the right place. To check whether your explanation is understandable and accurate, have someone read your paragraph and then draw a chart or map, pointing out exactly what he or she understands the route to be. If the person makes a mistake, try to figure out how to revise your explanation so that it won't be misunderstood.

## Intermediate Writing Assignment: How-to Paragraphs

Before writing your own paragraph, read the paragraph below, in which the authors explain how to use what they call Baby Signs, that is gestures that parents can use to communicate with infants before they can actually speak. Explain what kind of analysis the authors use to develop their main point. Identify the examples they give to make the procedure easier to follow.

Because you are using Baby Signs as a bridge to speech, it is important to say the word as you make the sign. Connecting the Baby Sign with the word for the child reinforces both. Keep in mind that using Baby Signs is a way to help your baby "talk" by providing him with a choice. When he hears the word and sees the sign he has two options available instead of only one. Some words, like *ball* or *up*, will be easier for your baby to say than others. In those cases, he may choose to learn the word right from the beginning. Other words, like *flower*, may be more difficult, and your baby may therefore choose to sign. By using Baby Signs and words together, you are leaving both doors open. What's more, even when your baby uses the sign first, he will be learning to understand what you are saying and will have a head start in figuring out how to say the word himself.

—Linda Acredolo, Ph.D., and Susan Goodwyn, Ph.D., *Baby Signs: How to Talk with Your Baby Before Your Baby Can Talk* (New York: McGraw-Hill, Contemporary Books, 2002), 43–4.

Now choose one of the following topics and write your own "how-to" paragraph. Remember to begin with a concise, clear topic statement and to develop your discussion step by step, using transitional words. First do a page of focused writing; then compose your paragraph. Revise and correct the final draft. Use both explanation and examples to develop your paragraph.

1. How to lose weight
2. How to behave during a job interview
3. How to choose a major in college
4. How to care for a cat
5. How to stop smoking
6. How to plan a wedding reception
7. How to plan a vacation

## Challenge Writing Assignment: Process Paragraphs

Write a paragraph on one of the following topics explaining a process or pattern of development. Remember to identify the stages of development by using such terms as *at first, soon, meanwhile, next, later,* and *finally.*

1. Explain how people become addicted to a particular substance.
2. Explain how people change when they become parents.
3. Explain how students change when they go to college.
4. Explain how communications technology has changed in the last ten years.

5. Explain how music styles have changed in the last ten years.
6. Explain how children change when they become adolescents.
7. Explain how immigrants adjust to living in the United States.

# Definition Paragraphs: Explaining a Term

Writing a paragraph defining a term means more than giving a dictionary definition. Instead, it means discussing the word—how it is used, what it means, and what it does not mean. More than that, it means analyzing the experience, relationship, object, or idea to which the word refers. Defining *love*, for instance, is a way of explaining how people relate to each other; defining *success* is a way of discussing what people try to achieve in our society. In a good definition, the writer includes examples, humor, or analysis to offer the reader a full sense of the concept behind the word itself. **Definition** paragraphs often follow a climactic sequence based on a point-by-point analysis or a series of examples, building up to the most important.

Topic sentences in definition paragraphs usually have two parts: The writer first identifies the word in a general category and then gives specific criteria for it. The rest of the paragraph then goes on to elaborate, by analysis and examples, on these criteria. Here is a one-sentence definition. Notice the category and the specific description.

*general category*    *specific information about the subject*

A *shortstop* is a baseball player who stands between second and third base and catches ground balls, line drives, and short fly balls.

---

**WRITING EXERCISES:** Basic, Intermediate, Challenge

## Basic Exercise: Definition Paragraphs

Circle the general category in each definition and underline the specific criteria.

1. *Terrorism* is a form of political violence intentionally aimed at civilians for the purpose of creating fear in a whole population.
2. A *prerequisite* is an academic requirement, such as a previous class or test score, that students must satisfy before registering for a course.

3. A *sonnet* is a lyrical poem made up of fourteen lines and usu-ally built on a traditional rhyme scheme in the English or Italian mode.

4. A *soft sell* is a sales technique in which the salesperson uses tricky psychological methods to persuade the customer.

5. A *browser* is a software program used to look at various resources on the Internet.

6. A *caucus* is a meeting of a political group to discuss and decide on plans, candidates, or strategies.

7. A *primary* is an election in which each party chooses a candidate to run in the general election.

## Intermediate Exercise: Definition Paragraphs

Definition paragraphs begin with one-sentence definitions and dis-cuss the characteristics or parts of the thing being defined. You can see how the definitions just given could easily become topic sentences for whole paragraphs. Each needs examples or explanations to help the reader understand the term better. If we begin by defining *terror-ism* as a form of political violence directed at civilians, we could go on to give examples of terrorists in different parts of the world and describe their methods.

Write one-sentence definitions for seven of these terms. For each term, name the general category into which it fits and its specific characteristics, purpose, or function.

| | | |
|---|---|---|
| film director | blog | Ipad |
| role model | hip-hop | elective course |
| superstar | bureaucrat | gridlock |
| computer virus | antidepressant | green card |

## Challenge Exercise: Definition Paragraphs

Before writing your own definition paragraph, read the following paragraph written by the economist Michael Zweig in which he de-fines the term *class*.

Classes are groups of people connected to one another, and made different from one another, by the ways they interact when producing goods and services. This production process is based in the workplace, but extends into the political and cultural dynamics of society as well, where the rules and expectations that guide the economy are laid down, largely in accord with the needs of the economically powerful. Class is not a box that we "fit" into, or not, depending on our own personal attributes. Classes are not isolated and self-contained. What class we are in depends upon the role we play, as it relates to what others do, in the complicated process in which goods and services are made. These roles carry with them different degrees of income and status, but their most fundamental feature is the different degrees of power each has. The heart of class is not about lifestyle. It is about economics.

—Michael Zweig, *The Working Class Majority: America's Best Kept Secret* (Ithaca and London: Cornell University Press, 2000), 11.

What common ideas about class does the author reject in this paragraph? How does his definition of *class* differ from the way many people interpret the meaning of the term? Use your own analytical skills to write a paragraph defining one of the terms below. Begin with a sentence identifying the general category, and then develop your definition by analyzing and giving examples of the concept. As part of your explanation, you may want to refute false or commonly held but misguided ideas about the concept, as in the paragraph above. Remember: This is not simply a dictionary definition, but an interesting, even controversial, *explanation* of the term.

| | | |
|---|---|---|
| creativity | heroism | freedom |
| beauty | intelligence | racism |
| marriage | education | individualism |
| friendship | feminism | success |

## Classification: Dividing into Categories

A paragraph can break down a large subject into categories. Writing **classification** paragraphs in which your group subjects into categories is useful practice in thinking and organizing. Your main groups should belong in the same overall category but not overlap. Read the following sample paragraph, noticing the use of transitional words and the clear separation of categories.

## Sample Paragraph

*There are three main kinds of addiction: dependency on chemical substances, on patterns of activity or behavior, and on people. Addiction of the first type is familiar to everyone in the form of drug addiction and alcoholism. However, it also includes dependency on such substances as tobacco, coffee, and sedatives. Addiction to patterns of behavior includes excessive television watching, playing video games, gambling, eating, exercising, and sleeping. The third form of dependency is the immature reliance on and need for another person or persons, as opposed to a productive relationship in which both partners gain and contribute out of free choice. What characterizes all forms of addiction is an inability to function well without the habit, along with a destructive effect on the person's life and social relationships.*

This paragraph explains that there are three kinds of addiction, and that they have certain things in common. The purpose of dividing a subject into categories is to understand it better. In this case, we understand what makes addiction undesirable, even when the addiction is to a good thing, like a relationship or exercise. Sometimes we can see something clearly only when we identify its different types. In biology, we divide animals and plants into many categories by a system called **taxonomy.** Biologists can name the species, genus, and family to which a particular animal or plant belongs. Only by such a system is it really possible to understand living things, including human beings.

## Guidelines for Classification

**Choose categories that belong together but don't overlap.** To separate people or objects into categories, choose categories that are in the same general area. If you are categorizing types of narratives, for example, you might choose history, biography, and fiction as three kinds of books that tell stories. But you could not include Mexican books as a fourth type, because it is another kind of category: Mexican books could be found in all three categories. **Choose categories and examples that are on the same level.** If you were to write a paragraph based on geographical categories, for example, you might group the United States into regions, such as the

Northeast, the Midwest, the South, and so on. It would not make sense, however, to add a category such as large cities, rural counties, or other subgroups. In that case, Atlanta would belong in two groups. **Include only three or four categories in a paragraph.** You have probably seen the charts of plant and animal life in biology textbooks; these diagrams, which illustrate the taxonomy of life forms, usually include hundreds of categories and subcategories. Writing a paragraph in which you classify people, things, or processes will succeed only if you focus on a few categories, usually three or four at most. Unlike a family tree or a taxonomic chart, your paragraph will zoom in on what makes a few categories separate from one another. **Distinguish each category clearly from the others.** Try to identify the essential quality of each category, giving a kind of mini-definition of that group. If you are writing about categories of domestic animals, for example, you might explain the purpose of each group—household pets kept for companionship, work animals bred and raised for specific tasks, animals raised to provide food, and animals trained for entertainment.

Try the following exercises to sharpen your powers of classification.

WRITING EXERCISES: Basic, Intermediate, Challenge

## Basic Exercise: Classification Paragraphs

Identify three main groups in which all the people in the following list can be placed. List all of them under the appropriate headings.

| | | |
|---|---|---|
| Michael Bloomberg | Tiger Woods | Colin Powell |
| David Beckham | Al Sharpton | Anne Hathaway |
| Martin Lawrence | Macaulay Culkin | Danica Patrick |
| Hugo Chávez | Billy Dee Williams | Peyton Manning |
| Meryl Streep | Angela Merkel | Usain Bolt |
| Barack Obama | Jennifer Aniston | Hillary Clinton |
| Sandra Oh | Halle Berry | Sarah Palin |
| LeBron James | Serena Williams | Janet Jackson |
| Wayne Gretzky | Angelina Jolie | Kobe Bryant |
| Julio Iglesias | Vladimir Putin | |
| Brad Pitt | Lawrence Fishburne | |

## Intermediate Exercise: Classification Paragraphs

Divide each of the following subjects into three categories—that is, identify three types of colleges, relationships, and so on. Do not let the categories overlap.

1. Forms of entertainment
2. Vehicles
3. Stores
4. Relationships
5. Colleges
6. Technological devices
7. News sources

## Challenge Exercise: Classification Paragraphs

Write a paragraph explaining the three main categories of one subject in the preceding list. First do a brainstorming list including as many examples as possible; then identify at least three main categories into which the examples fit. Write an exploratory draft describing these categories and providing an example of each. Read your paragraph aloud; write a final draft.

# Cause and Effect Paragraphs: Telling Why

Often in a college assignment you will have to analyze the **cause and effect** of something—inflation, wars, unemployment, drug addiction, scientific progress, or changes in fashion and artistic style. To write such examinations or term papers well, you will usually have to study the subjects and do research. To prepare now for such advanced writing, you can create paragraphs in which you explore causes and effects by using your own knowledge, experience, and ability to analyze. You can explore most issues intelligently without being an expert, but analysis requires more than expressing an opinion: You must support it with clear reasoning, facts, experience, and examples.

## *Guidelines for Cause and Effect Analysis*

**Don't assume.** Of course you already have an opinion before you start writing, but explore the topic with an open mind. Instead of settling for the first explanation that pops into your mind (usually the one that everyone comes up with), test it. Could it be wrong or partly wrong?

**Don't oversimplify.** Most important social problems and historical events have more than one cause. Consider indirect causes as well as immediate causes. Remember that something occurring *after* something else is not necessarily *caused by* it.

**Avoid the blame-game.** When discussing the causes of a problem, try not to blame everything on the convenient scapegoats. It's too easy to blame the media for every problem from poor student achievement to street gangs and drug addiction. How do we know what is really the cause? Could the media be only one of many causes? Which is the most important one?

**Do your homework.** If you write an analytical paper for a specialized course such as sociology or history, back up your statements with facts from assigned readings or research. The instructor is interested less in your personal opinion than in your conclusions based on an analysis of what you have read. Even in personal essays, look up facts if you need them.

---

WRITING ASSIGNMENT: Basic, Intermediate, Challenge

## Basic Writing Assignment: Cause and Effect Paragraphs

Write a paragraph explaining one of the following topics. Be sure to explore the many possible causes before settling on the most important one, and do some critical thinking about it. Remember to use transitional expressions to hold the paragraph together, especially terms like *therefore, consequently, so, nevertheless, however, in addition, as a result,* and *moreover.*

1. Explain why you entered college.
2. Explain why you chose your college major.
3. Explain why you are (or are not) married.
4. Explain why you belong to a particular organization.
5. Explain why you wear your hair the way you do.
6. Explain why you do (or do not) want to have children.
7. Explain why you live where you do.

## Intermediate Writing Assignment: Cause and Effect Paragraphs

In the following paragraph, the writer begins with a topic sentence and stays on the topic by discussing one cause of crime. In what way, however, does he fail in this first draft to make a thorough analysis of the problem?

> Poverty is the cause of crime. Poor people steal because they can't get money any other way. How can the government expect to get rid of crime when there are so many people without jobs or a decent income to live on? The cost of living keeps going up for poor people, and they have to go out and commit crimes to pay the rent and put food on the table. All the government has to do to eliminate the crime problem is provide jobs and housing for the poor. It's the government's fault that the crime rate keeps rising. People who have decent housing, food, and clothing do not commit crimes.

After getting feedback from readers, this writer discovered that he needed to make revisions, as many readers disagreed with some of his points. He realized that he had oversimplified the problem and made a scapegoat of the government. Not that he was completely wrong; he simply had to focus his argument better and support it with better reasoning.

Here is his revised paragraph.

> Poverty is often said to be the chief cause of crime. But the real cause cannot be poverty alone, since some very poor communities have little crime and since most poor people are not criminals. The greater problem is poverty in the midst of a rich society, a society in which crime has become a means of making quick money. Some people who become accustomed to a life of drug peddling, car stripping, or working for organized crime syndicates believe that they can rise out of poverty faster and farther through crime than by doing legitimate work. They look around and see many prosperous and some extremely rich people who got money quickly through Internet companies that ballooned and disappeared or even through investment frauds called Ponzi schemes; consequently, they want to grab the easiest money they can get. Crime has become a major "career," with a nationwide annual income of hundreds of billions of

dollars. As long as this situation continues, and as long as people born into poverty believe that crime offers a promising "occupation," the United States will continue to have an enormous amount of crime.

Write your own cause and effect paragraph. Do a page of focused writing on one of the topics from the list that follows. Look over your page and try to identify the precise cause or effect involved. Be sure that your explanation makes a convincing connection between the cause and the effect, and try to include an example or two. Remember to use transitional expressions to hold the paragraph together, especially terms like *therefore, consequently, so, nevertheless, however, in addition, as a result,* and *moreover.*

1. What caused a particular performer, performing group, or athletic team to succeed?
2. What is causing the high divorce rate?
3. What causes many students to drop out of high school (or college)?
4. What causes people to be religious?
5. What effect has the death of Osama bin Laden had on the United States?
6. What effect has hip-hop had on young people?
7. How does being rich affect a person?

## Challenge Writing Assignment: Cause and Effect Paragraphs

Read the paragraph below by Judith Harris and identify the cause and effect relationship explained in it. How does she use transitional expressions to achieve coherence? What extended example does she give and what does it illustrate? This paragraph explains what she calls "group socialization theory." Judging from this paragraph, explain what this theory probably argues.

Children get their ideas of how to behave by identifying with a group and taking on its attitudes, behaviors, speech, and styles of dress and adornment. Most of them do this automatically and willingly: they *want* to be like their peers. But just in case they have any funny ideas, their peers are quick to remind them of the penalties of being different. School-age children, in particular, are merciless in their persecution of the one who is different: the nail that sticks up gets hammered down. The hammering sometimes makes the child aware of what he's doing wrong and almost always motivates him to change it. Psycholinguist Peter Reich still cringes when he recalls a childhood experience at a Boy Scout Jamboree. He grew up in Chicago, where the word *Washington* was pronounced *Warshington*. Boy Scouts from other parts of the country would come up to him, ask him to say the name of the capital of the United States, and would "double up with laughter" when he did so. "I can still remember," says Reich, "practicing hard to change the pronunciation of this and other words that marked my dialect."

—Judith Harris, *The Nurture Assumption: Why Children Turn Out the Way They Do* (New York: The Free Press, 1998), 169–70.

Write your own cause and effect paragraph. Do a search on the Web to find out some information about one of the topics listed. Before writing, read several articles that give you facts that you didn't know. Then write a draft of a paragraph explaining what seems to be the most believable cause or effect on this topic. Be sure not to copy the exact words of any articles you read, whether in a book, magazine, or Web page. Do some focused writing on one of the topics from the list. Look over your page and try to identify the precise cause or effect involved. Be sure that your explanation makes a convincing connection between the cause and the effect. Remember to use transitional expressions to hold the paragraph together, especially terms like *therefore, consequently, so, nevertheless, however, in addition, as a result,* and *moreover.*

1. Explain the effects of prolonged use of marijuana.
2. Explain the psychological effects of pornography.
3. Explain the side effects of performance-enhancing drugs.
4. Explain the effects of being raised by gay parents.
5. Explain the cause of obesity in the United States.
6. Explain the cause of widespread depression among teenagers.
7. Explain the causes of high unemployment in our current economy.

# Persuasion: Writing to Convince

Writing that explains why the reader should believe something or why society should do something is called *persuasive writing.* In this kind of writing you are trying to change someone's opinion or give reasons why a particular opinion is correct. You will find persuasive writing in many places outside the classroom, such as political speeches and debates, editorials in newspapers, business reports that recommend new policies, attorneys' speeches in court, advertising of all kinds, and books that advocate changes in laws, policies, or attitudes. These kinds of persuasive writing and talking can range from a few words to a whole book. In writing persuasive paragraphs, you will develop skills that carry over to many other situations.

Every attempt at persuasion can be boiled down to one topic sentence. The speaker or writer argues that something *should* or *ought* to be done. Persuasive paragraphs frequently use words like *should, ought, might, must, have to, could, probably, likely, possibly, certainly,* and *undoubtedly*. Such words measure what the writer thinks should be changed in people's attitudes or actions. These words signal *why* relationships—causes, effects, and consequences. They link motives and reasons to actions. Learn to use them correctly in your own paragraphs.

## Guidelines for Persuasive Writing

**Be sure your topic sentence states an opinion.** If you begin your paragraph with a sentence that merely states a fact, it may never be clear to your reader or even to yourself what you are arguing. Your paragraph may wander around the topic while the reader is impatiently waiting for you to get to the point. A sentence like "Immigration is an important subject nowadays" is not a persuasive statement; it does not express your opinion about immigration. "Undocumented immigrants should (or should not) be granted amnesty" does express an opinion.

**State your opinion firmly and clearly, but don't overgeneralize.** If you make a forceful topic statement, the reader will know exactly where you stand. But it should be a careful, accurate statement and not exaggerated: If *most* people act a certain way, don't say that *everybody* does.

**Support your opinion with relevant arguments and facts.** You won't convince anyone if you keep restating your opinion without support. You have to give facts, reasons, examples, testimony (experts' opinions), and personal experience to build a strong case. Be sure as well that your supporting facts are relevant to your argument.

**Be logical and fair; avoid being dogmatic.** It's tempting to jump to conclusions, ignore facts that don't support your opinion, and pretend to know everything. Arguing dogmatically, the way some radio talk-show hosts sneer at those who disagree with them, can be emotionally satisfying to those who already share your opinion, but it will not convince open-minded thinkers.

**Remember your readers.** If they disagree, they are not necessarily stupid, so don't insult them. Consider what they might be thinking and try to answer their objections. You won't weaken your point by showing that you understand opposing views.

---

WRITING EXERCISES: Basic, Intermediate, Challenge

## Basic Exercise: Persuasive Writing

In each pair of sentences, explain which one is more persuasive and why. Tell what is wrong with the less persuasive one and which of the above guidelines it ignores.

1. Which statement is more persuasive?
   A. Marijuana is sometimes used for medical purposes.
   .B. Medical marijuana should be legalized in all states because it is effective in alleviating pain.
2. Which statement is more persuasive?
   A. Every student should have to take one course online because Professor Adams is a great teacher.
   B. Every student should have to take an online course because online courses provide a different kind of experience than traditional classes do.
3. Which statement is more persuasive?
   A. Women can be effective police officers. Commissioners' reports from five major cities show that female officers have performed as well as male officers.
   B. Women can never be good police officers; police work is not women's work.
4. Which statement is more persuasive?
   A. Anyone who opposes building the new gymnasium should look at the shabby and hazardous condition of the old one.
   B. Anyone who opposes building the new gymnasium is a traitor to the college.

5. Which statement is more persuasive?
   A. You should eat oatmeal for breakfast because it lowers your cholesterol.
   B. You should eat oatmeal for breakfast because it has the greatest television ads.
6. Which statement is more persuasive?
   A. This is a great novel because it is easy to read.
   B. This is a great novel because it gives an inspiring account of ordinary people overcoming terrible obstacles.
7. Which statement is more persuasive?
   A. Sharon needs a car because most of her friends own cars.
   B. Sharon needs a car because the buses and trains don't stop near her job.

## Intermediate Exercise: Persuasive Writing

Identify which of the following two paragraphs gives more effective support for the topic statement. Explain what the weaker one needs to make it more persuasive.

### Paragraph A

To find the right person for you, use your computer. It's a cool way to find somebody, and lots of people have been doing it. There are other ways to try to find Mr. or Ms. Right, but doing it on the Web is the best. Lots of people have met their wives or husbands by using matching services and they really benefited from it. It's all right to go out on blind dates, but you'll have better luck using computer Match-Ups.

### Paragraph B

Using a personal matching service on the Web is the best way to meet the partner of your dreams. On the Web you can match information on the person's work, education, political views, favorite activities, and preferences in music, food, and literature and compare them with your own. You know that before you even meet, you have more in common than most married people, and you know as much about each other as most people take months to discover. Some people might object that knowing so much ahead of time takes the risk and excitement out of meeting the person. But it really doesn't because no matter how much you know and how well matched you are, there is always a question of personal chemistry, the mysterious feelings people have about each other that cannot be fed into a database. The advantage is that you have a much better chance of meeting a person who wants what you want and enjoys what you enjoy. How often does that happen through chance meetings or blind dates? Instead of having a friend guess that a certain person is right for you, you can figure out for yourself whether the match-up is likely to succeed. That, at least, is what I am told by three couples who met their spouses through Web matching services. They all insist they could never have met anyone as compatible through casual dating or in any other way. One couple even said they both had almost given up hope of ever finding someone who shared their tastes and attitudes.

## Challenge Exercise: Persuasive Writing

Explain whether each of these sentences seems persuasive. If not, explain what is wrong with it, and rewrite the sentence to make it more persuasive. In each sentence, identify the conclusion reached and the evidence or claim given to support it. In each case, ask yourself the following questions.

- Is the claim or evidence true?
- Does it actually support the conclusion?
- If it is true and supports the conclusion, is it adequate, or is more evidence needed?
- If the evidence does not make the conclusion convincing, what kind of evidence would make it convincing, or how could the conclusion be reworded to make it convincing?

1. The testimony must be false because it was given by a police officer, and police officers always lie on the witness stand.
2. You should get some advice from an experienced money manager before investing a lot of money because inexperienced investors often make big mistakes.
3. Young people should not follow their parents' advice because the world has changed a lot since their parents were young.
4. Cigarettes should be made illegal because smoking harms people's health.
5. Beverly would make a good lawyer because she likes to help people.

6. The new situation comedy is excellent: the acting is outstanding, the events are believable, and the dialogue is hilarious.

7. Eileen must have better taste than Judy because Eileen shops at more expensive stores.

## Basic Exercise II: Persuasive Paragraphs

Here are the beginnings of some *why* statements and *should* statements that could serve as topic sentences for persuasive paragraphs. Complete each sentence with a specific phrase that would serve as a guide for a persuasive paragraph.

1. College students should have credit cards because _____.
2. Bystanders who witness a violent crime should _____.
3. Learning to perform music is valuable because _____.
4. A teenager who wants to drink and use drugs ought to _____.
5. Learning to speak Spanish is a good idea because _____.
6. Working while attending high school is a good idea because _____.
7. Friends should (should not) exchange birthday presents because _____.

## Intermediate Exercise II: Persuasive Paragraphs

Identify the weakness of each statement below and explain how you would change it to make it a better beginning for a persuasive paragraph.

1. The death penalty should be imposed in all states because all the criminals are getting away with murder.
2. This is a great netbook because it costs more than any other item in the store.
3. This film will win the Academy Award because it has my favorite actress in it.
4. This witness must be telling the truth because he used to be a minister.
5. My diet is the best one for losing weight because I lost two pounds last week.
6. Teaching reading by the phonics method is best because everyone knows it works better than other methods.
7. Science courses should be required of all students because they are very interesting.

# Challenge Exercise II:
# Persuasive Paragraphs

Here are the beginnings of some *why* statements and *should* statements that could serve as topic sentences for persuasive paragraphs. Complete each sentence with a specific phrase that would serve as a guide for a persuasive paragraph, and give one supporting reason for each statement.

1. For college admissions, SAT scores should be _____ because _____.
2. Students for whom English is a second language should _____ because _____.
3. The best way for the U.S. to provide affordable medical care would be to _____ because _____.
4. Elections can be made fairer by _____ because _____.
5. To reduce the control of neighborhoods by gangs, cities should _____ because _____.
6. To protect us from terrorism, the government should _____ because _____.
7. College sports should be _____ because _____.

---

WRITING ASSIGNMENT: Basic, Intermediate, Challenge

# Basic Writing Assignment:
# Persuasive Paragraphs

Write a paragraph in which you try to persuade the reader to take one of the actions below. Begin with a topic sentence in which you take a clear, firm position and give a strong reason to agree with it. Develop your argument with analysis, facts, or examples.

1. Buy a product you like
2. Join an organization to which you belong
3. Attend your college
4. Listen to your favorite album
5. Register for your favorite course
6. Acquire the kind of pet you own
7. Live in a neighborhood you like

## Intermediate Writing Assignment: Persuasive Paragraphs

Read the following two case studies. Think about all the options faced by the people in each case. Analyze the pros and cons of each alternative. Choose one of the case studies, and write a paragraph in the form of a letter to the person in the case and try to persuade him or her to follow your recommendation.

### Case 1

Ms. Diaz is the principal of a high school in a metropolitan area. One group of students has come to her requesting that the school establish a club for gay students and create sensitivity workshops raising other students' awareness of gay issues. A second group has come to Ms. Diaz asking that she not accept the other group's proposal but instead establish a group for religious students so that they can participate in religious activities after classes are over. Ms. Dias respects both groups of students and finds some educational value in both proposals, but she also knows that if she accepts either one, some parents and community leaders will object. Write a paragraph advising her what to do.

### Case 2

Lauren and Patrick have been married four years and live in New Jersey. Both have career ambitions: He is a high school teacher, and she works for a large educational testing company. They both want to have children within a few years. Lauren's firm wants to promote her and move her to Iowa, where she will be in charge of a new project and have a higher salary with improved benefits. Patrick is confident that if they move to Iowa he will eventually get a teaching job, but he likes his current position. Lauren really wants to accept her company's offer. Write a paragraph advising Lauren or Patrick what to do.

## Challenge Writing Assignment: Persuasive Paragraphs

Write a persuasive paragraph answering one of the questions to follow. Begin with a topic sentence that takes a position and gives a strong reason to support it. Then explain why your position is right, using analysis, facts, or examples. Use transitional words like *therefore, but, in addition, consequently, however, of course, for example,* and *furthermore.*

1. Should cigarette smoking be banned in residential buildings?
2. Should 16-year-olds be allowed to drink?
3. Should people be allowed to keep dangerous animals as pets?
4. Should trials be televised?
5. Should two years of college be provided free?
6. Should computer applications be a required course for all students?
7. Should undocumented immigrants be allowed to have drivers' licenses?

## Key Words from Chapter 4 for Review

cause and effect, chronological sequence, classification, climactic sequence, comparison, comparative markers, definition, descriptive, expository, first person, narrative, narrative writing, past tense, persuasive, procedural writing, process analysis, rhetorical mode, spatial sequence, taxonomy, third person, time markers, time sequence, transitional expressions

# Some Added Features of Paragraph Writing

---

## STEPPING UP: WRITING TIP 5

Good writing requires clear and original thinking. In addition to mastering the modes of paragraph writing, you should learn to think both critically and creatively so that your writing will convey interesting and worthwhile ideas to your readers. In an age when so much that we see on television and read on the Internet tempts us to react unthinkingly and uncritically, it is more important than ever to make a conscious effort to think clearly. Thinking critically is not just being negative. It means analyzing carefully many issues that usually don't break down into simple good and evil, right and wrong. Positive solutions often come from the most careful critical and creative thinking.

---

## Critical Thinking in Paragraphs

**Critical thinking** means analysis based on evidence and reasoned judgment. No one is completely free of **biases** and **prejudices.** Clear critical thinking nevertheless requires us to put aside our biases while looking carefully at all sides of a problem or argument. You should develop the ability to think critically in all of your college courses, not just in writing courses, and this ability will in turn strengthen your writing.

When you write an expository or persuasive paragraph, try always to keep an open mind, sort out the different sides of the case, gather all the evidence, and make your point based on that evidence. It may take several drafts for you to arrive at a satisfactory analysis; don't jump to conclusions. In order to avoid dogmatic, one-sided thinking, read your work aloud to someone else, preferably someone with a different perspective on the problem than yours—you'd be surprised how much you can learn from someone else, even when you think your mind is totally made up!

---

WRITING ASSIGNMENT: Basic, Intermediate, Challenge

## Basic Writing Assignment: Critical Thinking in Paragraphs

Write a paragraph in which you disagree with an opinion most of your friends support. Explain why their opinion is not based on evidence, fact, and reason, and analyze why they have that opinion. Cite the facts and evidence that prove their opinion to be wrong.

## Intermediate Writing Assignment: Critical Thinking in Paragraphs

Write a paragraph on one of the topics that follow.

**Topic A:** Describe what you think is the best course given at your college. Analyze why it is such a good course and explain how it benefits students who take it. It will be easier for you to write about a course you are taking or have already taken, but you could also write about a course that friends have told you about. First do some thinking or prewriting about how you should evaluate a course.

**Topic B:** Describe the best store or restaurant in your neighborhood. Analyze why it is such a good establishment and how it benefits customers. First do some thinking or prewriting about how a store or restaurant should be evaluated.

## Challenge Writing Assignment:
## Critical Thinking in Paragraphs

Write a paragraph on one of the topics that follow.

**Topic A:** Look carefully at the table that follows and explain what it tells you about the incomes of different types of U.S. households.

### Median Income of Households by Selected Characteristics, 2009*

| Type of Household | Number of Households | Median Income |
|---|---|---|
| All households | 117,538,000 | $49,777 |
| Family households | 78,833,000 | $61,265 |
| Married-couple families | 58,410,000 | $71,830 |
| Female householder, no husband | 14,843,000 | $32,597 |
| Male householder, no wife | 5,580,000 | $48,084 |
| Nonfamily households | 38,705,000 | $30,444 |
| Female householder | 20,442,000 | $25,269 |
| Male householder | 18,236,000 | $36,611 |
| **Nativity of Householder** | | |
| U.S. Native | 103,039,000 | $50,503 |
| Foreign born | 15,449,000 | $43,923 |
| Naturalized citizen | 7,834,000 | $51,975 |
| Not a citizen | 7,666,000 | $36,089 |

*Source: U.S. Bureau of Census, *Income, Poverty, and Health Insurance Coverage in the United States: 2009*. Web source: www.census.gov.

**Topic B:** Look carefully at the table that follows and explain what it tells you about the connection between sports teams' success and their finances.

## Creative Thinking in Paragraphs

The power to think creatively is partly a gift. Some people just seem to have it, but anyone can develop it. Creativity in writing involves both your use of language and your ideas. Critical thinking is about

## 2010 American League
## Team Standings

| | Team | Wins | Losses | Ties | WP | GB | Payroll |
|---|---|---|---|---|---|---|---|
| **East** | Tampa Bay Devil Rays | 96 | 66 | 0 | .593 | — | $71,923,471 |
| | New York Yankees | 95 | 67 | 0 | .586 | 1 | $206,333,389 |
| | Boston Red Sox | 89 | 73 | 0 | .549 | 7 | $162,747,333 |
| | Toronto Blue Jays | 85 | 77 | 0 | .525 | 11 | $62,689,357 |
| | Baltimore Orioles | 66 | 96 | 0 | .407 | 30 | $81,612,500 |
| | **Team** | **Wins** | **Losses** | **Ties** | **WP** | **GB** | **Payroll** |
| **Central** | Minnesota Twins | 94 | 68 | 0 | .580 | — | $97,559,167 |
| | Chicago White Sox | 88 | 74 | 0 | .543 | 6 | $108,273,197 |
| | Detroit Tigers | 81 | 81 | 0 | .500 | 13 | $122,864,929 |
| | Cleveland Indians | 69 | 93 | 0 | .426 | 25 | $61,203,967 |
| | Kansas City Royals | 67 | 95 | 0 | .414 | 27 | $72,267,710 |
| | **Team** | **Wins** | **Losses** | **Ties** | **WP** | **GB** | **Payroll** |
| **West** | Texas Rangers | 90 | 72 | 0 | .556 | — | $55,250,545 |
| | Oakland Athletics | 81 | 81 | 0 | .500 | 9 | $51,654,900 |
| | Los Angeles Angels of Anaheim | 80 | 82 | 0 | .494 | 10 | $105,013,667 |
| | Seattle Mariners | 61 | 101 | 0 | .377 | 29 | $98,376,667 |

Source: *Baseball Almanac.* Web source: http://www.baseball-almanac.com/yearly/yr2010a.shtml.

analyzing a problem put before you and seeing its parts in relation to one another, about weighing the evidence. **Creative thinking** requires something more—coming up with proposals and solutions that haven't already been thought of. Sometimes this is called lateral thinking or "thinking outside the box." Until an original thinker comes along, problems can seem unsolvable. Once he or she sees an original solution, the idea soon seems obvious. Such are scientific discoveries, and the same is true in music, art, and literature. New ideas seem strange at first, but once we become familiar with them, it's hard to believe they weren't obvious to everyone.

In your writing, try to exercise your powers of creativity in your choice of words and your ideas. Avoid clichés, that is, the phrases and ideas that were funny, original, or moving the first time we heard them but quickly became boring. Don't be afraid to try out a new idea or a different phrase of your own.

---

WRITING ASSIGNMENT: Basic, Intermediate, Challenge

## Basic Writing Assignment: Creative Thinking in Paragraphs

Write a paragraph on one of the topics that follow. First, brainstorm several possible ideas before you decide on the best one. Then write a draft and read it aloud to another student. Revise your paragraph to strengthen your support of your main point and make final corrections.

**Topic A:** Visualize yourself ten years from now. Describe where you hope to be living and what you hope to be doing. Explain how your personal circumstances, education, and work will change by that time and how you will experience the change.

**Topic B:** Imagine yourself as a different kind of person, that is, a person of a different national, ethnic, or religious background, a different historical period, or of the opposite sex. Describe what your life would be like if you could be such a person, and explain why you would or would not like to be that kind of person.

## Intermediate Writing Assignment: Creative Thinking in Paragraphs

Write a paragraph on one of the topics that follow. First, brainstorm several possible ideas before you decide on the best one. Then write a draft and read it aloud to another student. Revise your paragraph to strengthen your support of your main point and make final corrections.

**Topic A:** Your college has been given $10 million by a wealthy graduate. She wants the money to be used to improve the quality of education at the school through the use of technology. Write a paragraph proposing how the money should be spent, explaining why your proposal would maximize the educational benefits of the gift.

**Topic B:** A study of student satisfaction at your college has revealed that a large number of students are not happy with their social experience at the school. Write a paragraph in which you propose one change that would most improve the way students relate to one another at the college. Visualize and describe the way the school will be when those changes have been made.

## Challenge Writing Assignment: Creative Thinking in Paragraphs

Write a paragraph on one of the two topics below. Be as resourceful as you can in coming up with interesting ideas and ways of expressing your thoughts. Be sure to try out your paragraph on other readers and revise your draft.

**Topic A:** The paragraph below was written by a famous writer who grew up in Antigua, West Indies. In it, a parent or grandparent (most likely a mother) is speaking to a girl about how she should behave. Read the paragraph carefully and notice how the parent talks to the girl and what she says to her. Then write a paragraph created from your own observation of how the older and younger generations relate to each other. Write the paragraph from the point of view of a parent in the United States today—either a father or a mother—telling a son or daughter how to behave.

# Girl

JAMAICA KINCAID

Wash the white clothes on Monday and put them on the stone heap; wash the color clothes on Tuesday and put them on the clothesline to dry; don't walk barehead in the hot sun; cook pumpkin fritters in very hot sweet oil; soak your little cloths right after you take them off; when buying cotton to make yourself a nice blouse, be sure that it doesn't have gum on it, because that way it won't hold up well after a wash; soak salt fish overnight before you cook it; is it true that you sing benna in Sunday school?; always eat your food in such a way that it won't turn someone else's stomach; on Sundays try to walk like a lady and not like the slut you are so bent on becoming; don't sing benna in Sunday school; you mustn't speak to wharf-rat boys, not even to give directions; don't eat fruits on the street—flies will follow you; *but I don't sing benna on Sundays at all and never in Sunday school;* this is how to sew on a button; this is how to make a buttonhole for the button you have just sewed on; this is how to hem a dress when you see the hem coming down and so to prevent yourself from looking like the slut I know you are so bent on becoming; this is how you iron your father's khaki shirt so that it doesn't have a crease; this is how you iron your father's khaki pants so that they don't have a crease; this is how you grow okra—far from the house, because okra tree harbors red ants; when you are growing dasheen, make sure it gets plenty of water or else it makes your throat itch when you are eating it; this is how you sweep a corner; this is how you sweep a whole house; this is how you sweep a yard; this is how you smile to someone you don't like too much; this is how you smile to someone you don't like at all; this is how you smile to someone you like completely; this is how you set a table for tea; this is how you set a table for dinner; this is how you set a table for dinner with an important guest; this is how you set a table for lunch; this is how you set a table for breakfast; this is how to behave in the presence of men who don't know you very well, and this way they won't recognize immediately the slut I have warned you against becoming; be sure to wash every day, even if it is with your own spit; don't squat down to play marbles—you are not a boy, you know; don't pick people's flowers—you might catch something; don't throw stones at blackbirds, because it might not be a blackbird at all; this is how to make a bread pudding; this is how to make doukona; this is how to make pepper pot; this is how to make a good medicine for a cold; this is how to make a good medicine to throw away a child before it even becomes a child; this is how to catch a fish; this is how to throw back a fish you don't like, and that way something bad won't fall on you; this is how to bully a man; this is how a man bullies you; this is how to love a man, and if this doesn't work there are other ways, and if they don't work don't feel too bad about giving up; this is how to spit up in the air if you feel like it, and this is how to move quick so that it doesn't fall on you; this is how to make ends meet; always squeeze bread to make sure it's fresh; *but what if the baker won't let me feel the bread?*; you mean to say that after all you are really going to be the kind of woman who the baker won't let near the bread?

*benna:* popular music such as calypso
*doukona:* a dish common in the Caribbean
*dasheen:* Caribbean plant

**Topic B:** Read the following passage by the Argentinean writer Jorge Luis Borges. You may want to look up the meaning of several words, especially *engender, vagaries,* and *ephemeral.* Notice both the author's careful choice of details and his creative use of memory. Think of an object, creature, place, or image that has been a frequent presence in your imagination. Write a creative paragraph visualizing this phenomenon as you have imagined it. Be sure to use descriptive language creatively, and use your thesaurus to find the most precise and vivid words.

# Dreamtigers

## JORGE LUIS BORGES

In my childhood I was a fervent worshiper of the tiger—not the jaguar, that spotted "tiger" that inhabits the floating islands of water hyacinths along the Paraná and the tangled wilderness of the Amazon, but the true tiger, the striped Asian breed that can be faced only by men of war, in a castle atop an elephant. I would stand for hours on end before one of the cages at the zoo; I would rank vast encyclopedias and natural history books by the splendor of their tigers. (I still remember those pictures, I who cannot recall without error a woman's brow or smile.) My childhood outgrown, the tigers and my passion for them faded, but they are still in my dreams. In that underground sea or chaos, they still endure. As I sleep I am drawn into some dream or other, and suddenly I realize that it's a dream. At those moments, I often think: *This is a dream, a pure diversion of my will, and since I have unlimited power, I am going to bring forth a tiger.*

Oh, incompetence! My dreams never seem to engender the creature I so hunger for. The tiger does appear, but it is all dried up, or it's flimsy-looking, or it has impure vagaries of shape or an unacceptable size, or it's altogether too ephemeral, or it looks more like a dog or bird than like a tiger.

—Jorge Luis Borges, *Collected Fictions*, trans. Andrew Hurley (New York: Viking, 1998), 294.

# Including Quoted Text in Paragraphs

You can often strengthen your paragraphs, especially persuasive ones, by including **quotations.** Using quotations correctly is not very difficult if you understand the main rules.

**Inside quotation marks, write only the exact words of the original text.** That means, don't change a few words to suit your meaning and don't change an *I* to *he* or *she* to fit your previous sentence.

**EXAMPLE**

**Incorrect:** The author Joe Smith writes, "He disagrees with this argument."

**Correct:** The author Joe Smith writes, "I disagree with this argument."

Obviously, Joe Smith refers to himself as *I*, not *he.*

You may want to change this statement to **paraphrase,** as in the example that follows.

**Also correct:** The author Joe Smith believes that this argument is wrong.

Notice that the sentence above does not have quotation marks and is not considered a direct quotation.

**Introduce the quotation with a short phrase.** It is bothersome to a reader to see a pair of quotation marks appear out of nowhere. Identify the person you are quoting with an introductory phrase that we call a **signal phrase** or an **attributive tag,** meaning that you attribute the statement to someone. You may give the person's name or just refer to him or her as *one writer* or *the author* or *another expert.*

**EXAMPLES**

**Incorrect:** This article makes a false statement. "Nobody uses fax machines anymore."

**Correct:** In this article Joe Smith incorrectly states, "Nobody uses fax machines anymore."

**Incorrect:** Some children learn to read at the age of three. "There is no one right age for every child to begin reading."

**Correct:** Some children learn to read at the age of three. As psychologist Joe Smith writes, "There is no one right age for every child to begin reading."

**Use correct punctuation before quotations.** In the examples above, you will see a comma before every quotation. That is the usual punctuation. However, use a colon before a quotation which you introduce more formally, with phrases like *as follows* or *in the following words*.

**EXAMPLES**

**Incorrect:**  As one sportswriter insists "This was the best game of the tournament."

**Correct:**  As one sportswriter insists, "This was the best game of the tournament."

**Incorrect:**  One sportswriter summed up the outcome in the following words "This was the best game of the tournament."

**Correct:**  One sportswriter summed up the outcome in the following words: "This was the best game of the tournament."

**Note:** Sometimes you will want to quote just a few words or a phrase rather than a whole sentence. In such cases, you do not need a comma before the quoted words; just weave them smoothly into your sentence.

**EXAMPLE**

**Incorrect:**  The protesters called the decision an, "outrageous attack on free speech."

**Correct:**  The protesters called the decision an "outrageous attack on free speech."

**Capitalize the first word of a quoted sentence.** Treat the beginning of a quoted sentence just the way you do any other sentence; that is, begin it with a capital letter. This does not mean that a short quoted phrase woven into your sentence should be capitalized:

**EXAMPLES**

**Incorrect:**  The story begins, "**o**nce upon a time there was a princess."

**Correct:**  The story begins, "**O**nce upon a time there was a princess."

**Incorrect:**  The critic called the film "**A** pretentious failure."

**Correct:**  The critic called the film "**a** pretentious failure."

### TEST YOURSELF: Including Quoted Text in Paragraphs

Determine which of the following sentences use quotations correctly and which use quotations incorrectly. If a sentence contains an error or errors, explain what should be done to correct it.

1. The author of this essay writes, "She thinks capital punishment is wrong."
2. My sister always tells me that she hates to wear green.
3. As one psychologist writes, "many emotional disorders are partly genetic."
4. She asked the following question, "Who will manage the college's investments?"
5. The newspaper called the event a "Momentous change of direction."
6. Blueberries are good for your health. "Blueberries contain many nutrients."
7. One reviewer described the novel as "a masterpiece of brevity and humor."

*Answers:* 1. "I think . . . 2. correct 3. "Many . . . 4. question: 5. "momentous . . .
6. As one expert writes, "Blueberries contain . . . 7. correct

### WRITING EXERCISES: Basic, Intermediate, Challenge

## Basic Exercise: Including Quoted Text in Paragraphs

Two of the sentences below are correct. Find and correct the error in each of the other sentences.

1. Barbara said to her sister, "You are the only person who understands me."
2. Jay ended his story by writing, "the loser finally became a winner."
3. Eliza called the mathematics course an "Academic boot camp."
4. My aunt often gives me the following good advice. "Don't forget where you came from."
5. The sign at the intersection reads, "Turn right on red light."
6. The winner of the trophy said, "He couldn't have won without the support of others."
7. Stephanie asked "where she could find used books."

## Intermediate Exercise: Including Quoted Text in Paragraphs

Determine which of the following sentences use quotations correctly and which use quotations incorrectly. If a sentence contains an error or errors, explain what should be done to correct it.

1. The article makes the following statement, "the Supreme Court may consider the case."
2. The actor said "that he wants a different part in the film."
3. Preparations are being made for what the managers called "the sale of a lifetime."
4. The reader will ask, "Why does the main character not have a name."
5. The spokesperson for the company replied "Our policies have not changed."
6. "Wait until you see the results of the study" the economist declared.
7. Sharon made a good point about the course. "The textbook was hard but the exam was easy."

## Challenge Exercise: Including Quoted Text in Paragraphs

Determine which of the following sentences use quotations correctly and which use quotations incorrectly. If a sentence contains an error or errors, explain what should be done to correct it.

1. Albert Camus begins his novel *The Stranger* with the following words: "Mother died today. Or, maybe, yesterday; I can't be sure."
2. One sociologist argues that "he sees a connection between upward mobility and democracy."
3. Edwin Arlington Robinson's poem "Richard Cory" ends with the shocking statement "Went home and put a bullet through his head."
4. Doesn't the author of this article insist elsewhere that he is "opposed to all forms of capital punishment?
5. Samuel Taylor Coleridge describes our mind-set when we read poetry as a "willing suspension of disbelief."
6. One critic wrote "that the film was a crass exploitation of the public taste for cruelty and sensationalism."

7. Arthur Miller's play, *The Death of a Salesman*, ends with Willy Loman's wife Linda sobbing we're free. We're free."

## Key Words from Chapter 5 for Review

attributive tag, biases, creative thinking, critical thinking, paraphrase, prejudices, quotations, signal phrase

# Revising and Correcting Your Paragraphs

# Revising Your Paragraphs

---

## STEPPING UP: WRITING TIP 6

Learning to revise effectively lies at the heart of becoming a better writer. Most of the world's great authors revised their work many times. You may find revising difficult at first. You may resist making large changes in what you have written and concentrate instead on correcting small errors. With enough practice, however, you can become skillful at making big improvements in your work. Sometimes it is even better to write a paragraph over from the beginning to show yourself what changes are possible. Remember that making revisions is not a sign of bad writing but of setting high standards for yourself.

---

## Revising vs. Editing and Proofreading

Many beginning college writers aim for modest goals. They are satisfied with "good enough" paragraphs that will earn a passing grade. To create paragraphs that you will truly enjoy reading to classmates and friends, set your goals higher. Learn how to revise effectively, and visualize yourself writing paragraphs that will genuinely move and impress your readers.

Once you tap into your creative ability, you will become more ambitious about revision. It will become more than simply copying your first draft in neater handwriting or producing a second draft with a few surface touch-ups. **Revising** means *rethinking* the **content,** language, organization, and conception of your work. Revision requires far more deliberation and insightful judgment than **editing,** which is changing your writing so that it complies with the grammatical and conventional standards of written English, and **proofreading,** which is the act of finding surface errors in need of correction. When you revise, you engage with your writing at the deepest creative level, asking yourself whether your work has achieved your purpose, met the needs of your audience, and conveyed your message as effectively as possible.

Each experience of revision will be different. Sometimes a paragraph will need a complete rethinking of your purpose; at other times your paragraph will be too thin and need more facts and examples. Many paragraphs will need major improvements in language. Be ready to do real makeovers in any of these areas.

## A Student Writer at Work

Here is the first draft of a paragraph that Travis wrote and then revised extensively. He might have chosen not to revise his work: The paragraph isn't a poor piece of writing—there are only a few mechanical errors and Travis does make a point.

> *Having the right attitude about your body is important. Some people care too much about being overweight and turn into anorexics. Some people don't care at all and either get real obese or completely out of shape. Because they don't do any exercise. Some guys think only about being in great physical shape, they think looking like an Olympic athlete will get them anything. Some women spend all their time thinking about their diets and looking like models in fashion magazines. But there are some people who have the right attitude, they know how to keep their body image in perspective.*

But Travis didn't want to settle for a merely passable paragraph. After getting some responses from classmates, he decided that, although the paragraph had a good point and some development, he could make it more effective with some revisions. One reader told him that the point he developed was not what he said in his topic sentence: He began his paragraph by saying that the right attitude was important, but only gave examples of people with the wrong attitudes. Another classmate said that she thought his paragraph had good development but could use personal examples. Several readers found some mistakes in his use of language and some repetition in his sentences patterns. See if you can identify the mistakes and repetitions.

Travis decided to do a makeover of his paragraph keeping all these suggestions in mind. He thought of a more accurate topic sentence, improved and corrected his language, and included some additional examples. Here is his revised paragraph. Read it and answer the questions afterward, which focus on the kinds of improvements he made.

*If you want to have the right body image, there are two negative attitudes that you should avoid. One is to neglect your body completely. This attitude can cause you to become obese by eating too much unhealthy food or completely out of shape by never exercising. A friend of mine named Ted is only twenty-three but looks like he's forty-five because he parks at his computer all day and his only exercise is opening the refrigerator. He is already fifty pounds overweight. Another bad attitude is obsessing about your body. Some guys I know work out in the gym twenty-four/seven. They think having a great physique is more important than their jobs, their classes, or their families. Women tend to fuss about diets and dress sizes to the point that nothing else matters except looking like skinny models in fashion magazines. A cousin of mine was such a fanatic about losing weight that she had to be treated for anorexia. Both of these extremes, either ignoring your physical condition or concentrating on it all day long, will become destructive patterns. Steer clear of these attitudes and you can have a balanced, healthy life, mentally as well as physically.*

1. How did Travis change his topic sentence?
2. How did he reduce repetition in his sentence beginnings?
3. What personal examples did he add to the paragraph?
4. Find three errors in sentence construction in the first draft. Do they appear in the revision?
5. What two attitudes does Travis warn against in the paragraph?
6. Why is this paragraph more interesting than the first draft?
7. Is there anything you would recommend adding to this paragraph? Anything you would change?

## PEER REVIEW QUESTIONS

Use these questions to help you receive feedback from your classmates in revising your paragraphs. Although one reader can help you revise, getting feedback from a number of classmates is usually more valuable.

**Peer Review Worksheet**

1. Here is my impression of what you say in your paragraph:

2. You have a clear topic sentence.  ☐ Yes  ☐ No

3. You stay on the topic through the whole paragraph. ☐ Yes  ☐ No

4. You develop the topic  ☐ very well  ☐ sufficiently ☐ insufficiently.

5. I think your paragraph would benefit from the following kind(s) of revision:
   Rethinking your topic:  ☐ Yes  ☐ No
   Including more supporting material:  ☐ Yes  ☐ No
   Improving your style and grammar:  ☐ Yes  ☐ No

6. What I liked best about your paragraph is the following:

7. I recommend that you make the following changes:

# Altering Your Design

The most difficult kind of revision is rethinking your basic plan. Most of us, once we have written a paragraph, resist starting over. Sometimes, however, that's the best thing you can do with it. If you write on a computer, fortunately, you can save your first draft and work with a copy of it. That way you can revise freely without being afraid of losing the best parts of your first draft. Travis's original plan in his paragraph was to explain the right attitudes about body image, but after he wrote his draft, he realized his topic sentence didn't match the rest of his paragraph. He could rewrite his whole paragraph on the topic of the right attitudes, or he could rethink his plan and his topic sentence. That is what he did: He warned against two wrong attitudes and gave some examples. He had to change both his topic sentence and the rest of his paragraph.

# Enriching Your Content

Many inexperienced writers underestimate what a paragraph should contain and produce drafts that are as thin as skeletons. Don't be surprised if some of your peer reviewers recommend that you put more flesh on the bones by adding facts, details, or explanations to the draft of your paragraph. Travis added several personal examples to his paragraph to help the reader visualize the two types of wrong attitudes toward body image.

Find a paragraph you have already written and identify facts, ideas, or examples you can add to it to make it fuller, more persuasive, and more interesting. Make it a habit in the future to put more content into all of your drafts. Think of your paragraph in positive metaphors such as a landscape paintings crowded with colorful details, dinners with several courses of tasty foods, or theme parks with varied rides and activities. Provide your reader with a full experience, not just an abstract idea.

# Improving Your Style

You probably noticed that, in his second draft, Travis eliminated the boring **repetition** in his first draft, where almost every sentence has the phrase *some people* or *some guys* at or near the beginning. He worked toward **sentence variety**—changing sentence lengths and patterns to help maintain reader engagement. He also used words like *obsess, fuss about, fanatic, ignoring, steer clear, parks, anorexia,* and *concentrating.* By employing more powerful vocabulary, Travis made his paragraph more vibrant and interesting.

Take a close look at one of your best paragraphs and see whether you have been optimizing your use of rich vocabulary. Find words that you repeat too often and look in a thesaurus for synonyms of those words. Not all repetition is bad; a little of it, in fact, helps to hold your paragraph together. However, if you keep using the same word or phrase again and again, readers will notice it and find it boring.

Look at your sentence patterns, too. Do you always begin sentences the same way, and are they all the same length? Are you a choppy writer who always writes short, blunt sentences that march along without transitions? Or are you the rambling conversationalist who can never get to the end of a sentence? Notice your habits of **style**—certain mannerisms in the way you express yourself. No doubt you already have some habits of style that are effective, and you should develop your own voice. Achieving a strong, distinctive voice, however, isn't just doing what comes naturally. It is a combination of expressing your authentic self, noticing your language choices, and revising your style to make it concise and meaningful.

WRITING EXERCISES: Basic, Intermediate, Challenge

## Basic Exercise: Improving Your Style

Find a repeated word or phrase in each sentence and think of a substitute that is more vivid and specific.

1. Sarah looked impatiently through the manual and then realized she could look for the information more easily on the company's Web site.
2. Sidney went to the party at eight o'clock and stayed for two hours; then she went home.
3. The demonstration was very big; in fact, the crowd was so big that it filled the big plaza in the center of the city.
4. Melinda used to get angry all the time, but she has learned to control her anger by counting to ten whenever she starts to feel angry.
5. The coach is a really nice person, and the athletes work hard because she treats them nicely.
6. Jasmine and her brother are both good students, and, like most good students, they do good work in all of their courses.
7. The tour goes from Madrid to Barcelona; then it goes through southern France and goes back again to Madrid.

## Intermediate Exercise: Improving Your Style

In each group of sentences, change the beginning of one sentence to create variety.

1. The company did well last year, enjoying a 10 percent increase in sales. It did poorly this year, as the holiday sales dropped off. It will do better than ever next year, however.
2. Stanley completed his courses in December. He received his degree in February. He marched in the commencement exercises in June.
3. Yolanda became impatient waiting in the ticket line. She became even more frustrated having to empty her handbag and pass

through the metal detector. She almost went berserk waiting an hour for the plane to take off.

4. Hector thought he was ready to become a father for several reasons. He believed his marriage was stable because he and his wife had been together for five years. He also knew how to take care of a baby because he had taken care of his younger sister after she was born.

5. Teaching and learning are not the same thing. Teaching can be ineffective if the teacher does not make sure students are actually learning. Teaching can also be ineffective if students are measured by only one kind of test.

6. Priscilla received the package in mid-June, although it was mailed in May. Priscilla was excited even before she opened it. She knew it was from her cousin in Hawaii.

7. Janice was offered a free copy of her credit report by a credit card company. She decided to accept it because she was worried about her credit score. She thought she might apply for a mortgage if her credit was good enough.

## Challenge Exercise: Improving Your Style

Revise the paragraph below by (1) eliminating repetition, (2) substituting vivid, specific words for weak and vague words, and (3) rephrasing the sentences to make them more varied in length and form.

Congress passed a health care bill in 2010. Still, the American health care system needs more improvement. Millions of people are at risk because they can't afford medical insurance. Millions of others who have insurance may find out when they get sick that their coverage isn't good enough. Newspaper and magazine articles have made people see the need to fix the system. Michael Moore's 2007 film *Sicko* made people see how bad the problem is even though it made people laugh. Millions of people see a film like that and think the government should create a universal health care system. Millions of others see the film and think that private insurance companies and hospitals should fix the system. Other countries have less medical technology and fewer highly trained specialists. Many of them, though, manage to provide basic care for all of their people, rich or poor. There will continue to be disagreement about how to fix the system.

Almost everybody thinks the system needs to be fixed in some way. Politicians who opposed President Obama's health care plan should propose ways to improve it or to create a better plan if there is one.

## Key Words from Chapter 6 for Review

content, editing, proofreading, repetition, revising, sentence variety, style

CHAPTER

# Writing and Correcting Sentences

---

## STEPPING UP: WRITING TIP 7

Sentence mastery is based on the understanding of a few clear patterns. You should know the main parts of a simple sentence—the subject and verb—and understand how to connect simple sentences to create compound sentences. Creating complex sentences requires you to recognize independent and dependent clauses and to learn how to combine them correctly. Remember that simple sentences and clauses all contain a **subject**—the *what* or *who* that does the action—and a **verb**—the action word itself. Be sure to read your work aloud; this will help you identify sentence parts and spot errors.

---

## Writing Activities: Noticing Your Sentences

To concentrate on using sentences correctly and effectively, you will need plenty of your own writing to work with. You may use paragraphs you have already written, finding examples of grammatical features in your own work. Apply what you learn in the sentence exercises to your own paragraphs.

Keep on writing as you work on sentence structure. For more paragraph practice, choose five of the following topics and write at least one developed paragraph on each. Try to stay on topic and express your thoughts and feelings honestly; remember to include vivid details.

- Tell about a day in your life when something important happened. Follow the important event or events from beginning to end.
- Tell about a time when you changed in some way. Explain in detail how you changed and what caused the change to happen.
- Tell about a problem with which you had to cope. Tell how you tried to solve the problem and why you did or did not succeed.
- Tell about a relationship with a person who has influenced you. Describe the important things about that person in detail.
- Think of two key words that best describe you and explain how these qualities are exemplified in you.
- Describe your home to someone who has never met you. Use plenty of details to capture the important qualities of your home environment.
- Describe a place where you enjoyed being as a small child. Use plenty of details to help the reader use all five senses to share your experience.
- Tell about a trip you took with a friend or with your family. Describe in detail what you did and what you saw.

# Correcting Fragments

Examine the paragraphs you have just written to see if you have left any sentences incomplete. Incomplete sentences are usually called **fragments.** A fragment is a piece of something, like a rock chipped off a boulder. Often a sentence fragment is exactly that—a piece of a sentence that should be attached to the sentence before or after it, usually the one before. Fragments create a sense of incompleteness and interrupt the flow of your sentences.

**Attach a Fragment to the Previous Sentence.** You can often correct short, simple fragments by connecting them to the sentences before them.

**Fragment:**    Eloisa often asks questions in class. *And helps other students.*

**Correction:**    Eloisa often asks questions in class *and helps other students.*

**Attach a Fragment to the Sentence After It.** Sometimes a fragment must be attached to the sentence after it. In this case, you began a sentence, paused, wrote a period before you reached the end of the sentence, and continued on with a new sentence, leaving the fragment standing there.

| | |
|---|---|
| **Fragment:** | *Although the movie was exciting.* I liked the book better. |
| **Correction:** | *Although the movie was exciting,* I liked the book better. |

**Add a Subject or Verb to Turn a Fragment into a Whole Sentence.** You may also occasionally find a fragment that can't be attached to a sentence before or after it. This one will take a little more work. You'll have to add something to turn it into a complete sentence. Check it carefully: Does it have a subject? Does it have a verb? You'll probably have to insert one of these, sometimes both.

| | |
|---|---|
| **Fragment:** | The children in the new day care program. |
| **Correction:** | The children in the new day care program *made progress.* |
| **Fragment:** | After the training session, knew how to design a Web page. |
| **Correction:** | After the training session, *the students* knew how to design a Web page. |

---

### TEST YOURSELF: Correcting Fragments

Identify each item below as a complete sentence or fragment.

1. A person who believes that she can conquer the world.
2. Most immigrants work long hours at difficult jobs.
3. Because the holiday break begins on Thursday.
4. While waiting for the light to change.
5. The longest film I have ever seen.
6. When will the apartment be ready?
7. An assignment that is too difficult to finish in a week.

*Answers:* 1. fragment 2. sentence 3. fragment 4. fragment 5. fragment 6. sentence
7. fragment

## Basic Exercise: Correcting Fragments

Each pair may or may not contain a fragment. Correct all fragments by attaching them to the sentences before or after them.

1. The project is unpopular. And will cost too much.
2. Chemistry class is interesting. The lab is fun, too.
3. Tiffany spends her time in the mall. Looking for bargains.
4. Because the party was getting exciting. Julio didn't want to leave.
5. Sandra rearranged her schedule. To leave time for the meeting.
6. While campaigning for the student senate. Jason met his new girlfriend.
7. Matthew likes his new job. Especially the hours and salary.

## Intermediate Exercise: Correcting Fragments

Each pair may or may not contain a fragment. Correct all fragments by attaching them to the sentences before or after them.

1. Vanessa bought a new laptop computer. Which she needed for her travel business.
2. The company offered a new retirement plan. One that contained three options.
3. Not finding the dean in her office last Tuesday. Timothy returned the following Thursday.
4. Julia was not afraid of taking risks. For example, talking on her cell phone while driving.
5. Teenagers who drop out of school to work. Sometimes decide that they made a bad decision.
6. After each episode, viewers are left in suspense. Because of a surprise twist at the end.
7. May searched for information about cloning on the Web. She found interesting material.

## Challenge Exercise: Correcting Fragments

Each pair may or may not contain a fragment. Correct all fragments by attaching them to the sentences before or after them.

1. One thing remains clear to anyone who heard the lecture. That something needs to be done about the lack of accountability in the financial system.

2. The first child in a family usually has to assume responsibilities. Duties such as cooking, cleaning, and looking after the younger children.

3. Writing a good essay requires brainstorming, planning, and exploring your topic. As well as revising your work several times to make sure it is well written.

4. None of the colleges mentioned in the article appealed to Calvin. They all lacked programs in physical therapy, the career he wanted to pursue.

5. A slowdown in the economy can happen for various reasons. Such as jobs being sent overseas, higher oil prices, or fears of inflation.

6. There are many benefits that immigrants bring to the United States. Among them cultural diversity and a supply of talented workers.

7. Among the students taking online courses in science, government, and business last semester. Eighty percent completed the courses, and most reported that they learned as much as in the classroom.

## Overcoming ESL Problems: Using Subjects Correctly

Unlike some languages, English requires that you actually name the subject in every sentence. The only sentences from which the subjects are omitted are commands ("Look over to your left") or requests ("Please bring me a flash drive"). In these *imperative sentences*, as they are called, the word *you* is understood to be the subject.

In English, we cannot say, "Is raining" or "Is time for lunch," as in some languages. We say, "*It* is raining" or "*It* is time for lunch." We cannot say, "Is a good day for shopping." We say, "*This* is a good day for shopping." In some languages, the verb forms in such sentences indicate the subjects, but in English sentences of this type, the subjects must always appear.

**Pointer:** Be sure that you use "It is" with a singular statement, such as "It is a good idea to fasten your seat belt." Don't use it with a plural idea.

**Incorrect:**     *It is* many ways to get to Pittsburgh.

**Correct:**       *There are* many ways to get to Pittsburgh.

Neither is it correct in English to name the subject twice by using a pronoun after the noun subject.

**Incorrect:**     *My brother he* likes to play video games.

**Correct:**       *My brother* likes to play video games.

                   *He* likes to play video games.

---

### TEST YOURSELF: Using Subjects Correctly

In some of the following sentences, the subjects are missing. If the sentence is correct, write *C* in the blank. If the subject is missing, write an *X* over the place where the subject belongs, and in the blank write a word that would be a good subject. If the sentence has an incorrect double subject, cross out the extra one.

                              X
Example: _____it_____ The students thought was a difficult test.

Example: _____C_____ My sister belongs to a neighborhood church.

_____ 1. Gabriela she decided to ask her boss for a raise.

_____ 2. That is not the right answer to the question.

_____ 3. We stayed at home yesterday because was snowing.

_____ 4. Was not a good reason to knock him down.

_____ 5. The coach he was fired even though the team had a good year.

_____ 6. Sometimes will be hard to find the right Web site.

_____ 7. The book was hard to use because had no index.

*Answers:* 1. Gabriela decided 2. Correct 3. it was snowing 4. That was not
5. The coach was fired 6. it will be 7. because it had

---

### WRITING EXERCISES: Basic, Intermediate, Challenge

## Basic Exercise: Using Subjects Correctly

In some of the following sentences the subjects are missing. If the sentence is correct, write *C* in the blank. If the subject is missing, write an *X* over the place where the subject belongs, and in the blank write a word that would be a good subject. If the sentence has an incorrect double subject, cross out the extra one.

_____ 1. Hector he likes to work in the theater.

_____ 2. Is no reason to stay home when you can go with us.

_____ 3. Manuel drives well even when is raining or snowing.

_____ 4. Were plenty of ways to avoid a conflict.

_____ 5. The credit card company it never stops calling Allen.

_____ 6. Every month or two is a new store opening on the block.

_____ 7. The workshop was successful because was well planned.

## Intermediate Exercise: Using Subjects Correctly

In some of the following sentences the subjects are missing. If the sentence is correct, write C in the blank. If the subject is missing, write an X over the place where the subject belongs, and in the blank write a word that would be a good subject. If the sentence has an incorrect double subject, cross out the extra one.

_____ 1. The manager of the Philadelphia division he thinks it's important to hire more workers rather than demand overtime work from current employees.

_____ 2. Is obvious that there will have to be new ways for recording companies to ensure profits for themselves and incomes for their singers and instrumentalists.

_____ 3. Some of the members of the jury they did not think that the evidence presented by the prosecution was convincing.

_____ 4. Playing chess is challenging to students because trains them to concentrate and have patience.

_____ 5. Although a few Hollywood couples have remained together a long time, celebrity marriages usually don't last long.

_____ 6. Reality shows on television attract bigger audiences than situation comedies. Are popular in many countries and in fact were not invented in the United States.

_____ 7. Are many proposals for reforming the tax codes, which have become enormously complex.

## Challenge Exercise:
## Using Subjects Correctly

In some of the following sentences the subjects are missing. If the sentence is correct, write C in the blank. If the subject is missing, write an X over the place where the subject belongs, and in the blank write a word that would be a good subject. If the sentence has an incorrect double subject, cross out the extra one.

_____ 1. The history of social change it has been studied for two centuries since the time of the French Revolution.

_____ 2. Graduate schools of social work offer both master's degrees and doctorates, and are many undergraduate colleges where students can major in social work.

_____ 3. Have been many arguments put forward to explain the benefits of a core curriculum, which requires a prescribed set of courses in general education.

_____ 4. Many institutions collaborate in space exploration because it combines many kinds of scientific and technological expertise.

_____ 5. Mary Wollstonecraft Godwin she was one of the first writers to assert women's rights in an explicit manifesto.

_____ 6. Some of the biggest breakthroughs of the last decade have occurred in the field of genetics. Are likely to be even more spectacular discoveries in the next twenty years.

_____ 7. Inflation and unemployment they both play important roles in determining experts' analyses of the health of the national economy for the previous fiscal year.

# Run-on (Fused) Sentences

Every sentence should end with a period, exclamation point, or question mark. A **run-on sentence** occurs when a writer goes right through the end of the sentence like a driver going through a red light.

We saw Joanna duck behind a sales clerk obviously she didn't want us to recognize her.

In this sentence, *duck behind a sales clerk obviously* looks as if it goes together as a phrase, and it's easy to miss the cutoff point between sentences. Reading more carefully, we see that we have two sentences, not one:

We saw Joanna duck behind a sales clerk. Obviously she didn't want us to recognize her.

If two sentences are closely related, you may want to put them together in a compound sentence instead of separating them. Do not run them together, and do not put just a comma between them; use a semicolon, as in this sentence.

| | |
|---|---|
| **Run-on sentence:** | It took more than ten years to complete the reconstruction of the World Trade Center there were many financial and legal problems involved. |
| **Corrected as two separate sentences:** | It took more than ten years to complete the reconstruction of the World Trade *Center. There* were many financial and legal problems involved. |
| **Creating a compound sentence with a semicolon:** | It took more than ten years to complete the reconstruction of the World Trade *Center; there* were many financial and legal problems involved. |
| **Run-on sentence:** | The customers sent many e-mail messages to the company about its failure to deliver products on time however they did not receive any replies. |
| **Corrected as two separate sentences:** | The customers sent many e-mail messages to the company about its failure to deliver products on *time. However,* they did not receive any replies. |
| **Corrected with a semicolon:** | The customers sent many e-mail messages to the company about its failure to deliver products on *time; however,* they did not receive any replies. |

Identify each sentence as either correct or run-on.

1. Sandra strolled calmly into the classroom suddenly she gasped and hurried out.
2. The number of students who have applied to law school has increased it will go up even more next year.
3. Statistics courses are required in some majors; they give students useful skills in business and social science.
4. Modern poets experiment a lot with sound and imagery their verses are quite different from those of earlier poets.
5. Whatever Margie does, she always does thoroughly; she is a good role model.
6. After you see the film tell me about it reviewers said it is exciting.
7. Why isn't Jeremy here with us he promised to join us on the trip.

*Answers:* 1. RO 2. RO 3. C 4. RO 5. C 6. RO 7. RO

WRITING EXERCISES: Basic, Intermediate, Challenge

# Basic Exercise: Run-on Sentences

Find the spot at which each sentence is run together. Then explain how best to correct it. One sentence is correct.

1. Ben sent an e-mail message to Rita she didn't answer.
2. Linda placed her cell phone on the counter; suddenly it began to ring.
3. Aerobic exercises are boring to Maurice he prefers competitive sports.
4. Tracy is learning to make sushi she thinks it is easy.
5. Irish dancing appeals to Michael it is fast and dramatic.
6. Terry waited for the next train it arrived ten minutes late.
7. Roberta works for the Board of Education she wants to become a teacher.

# Intermediate Exercise: Run-on Sentences

Find the spot at which each sentence is run together. Then explain how best to correct it. One sentence is correct.

1. Books that become bestsellers are usually about current events and fashionable topics some bestsellers continue to interest readers for many years.

2. The film director spent years convincing the author and the producer to bring the novel to the screen she identified personally with the story.

3. Your cover letter should be long enough to show your serious intention it should not exceed two pages.

4. Terrorism has reduced tourism in certain countries; others, where terrorism is less frequent, have seen a corresponding increase in foreign visitors.

5. The distinction between professional and amateur athletes has almost disappeared in some sports perhaps we should eliminate it altogether.

6. Accidents in electrical plants can cause widespread power failures sometimes whole regions of the country can lose electricity.

7. Newspapers have to compete with television and the Internet therefore they try hard to make optimal use of their online editions.

## Challenge Exercise: Run-on Sentences

Find the spot at which each sentence is run together. Then explain how best to correct it. One sentence is correct.

1. Statistical analysis can be accurate in gauging such matters as population trends it is less reliable as a means of settling hotly debated political and social questions.

2. Immigration involves the states as well as the federal government. Although the states are responsible for educational, medical, and employment policies regarding immigrants, the Congress and the President make the immigration laws themselves.

3. Advice given to new parents by the experts changes with each generation psychologists' recommendations swing from strictness to permissiveness and back again.

4. Gerontology will continue to expand as a career and a subject of study the number and percentage of people over 65 has been increasing steadily.

5. Most colleges and universities offer a dozen or more modern languages some even offer as many as thirty.

6. Literature read in translation always loses something found in the original translations do however make possible a comparison of fiction, drama, and poetry from many cultures.

7. Interdisciplinary courses lead students to insights into separate disciplines as well as relations between disciplines such courses succeed best with students who are beyond the introductory level in the subjects involved.

# Comma Splices

Do not try to correct run-on sentences by inserting commas instead of periods. Such errors are called **comma splices.** Note the examples that follow.

| | |
|---|---|
| **Run-on sentence:** | More than fifty exquisite paintings were presented at the auction all but a few were sold within the first hour. |
| **Comma-spliced sentence:** | More than fifty exquisite paintings were presented at the auction, all but a few were sold within the first hour. |

Correct comma splices the same way you would correct run-on sentences. Separate the main clauses with a period or semicolon.

| | |
|---|---|
| **Corrected as two separate sentences:** | More than fifty exquisite paintings were presented at the auction. All but a few were sold within the first hour. |
| **Corrected with a semicolon:** | More than fifty exquisite paintings were presented at the auction; all but a few were sold within the first hour. |

## Coordinating Conjunctions

A third way to correct either run-on sentences or comma-spliced sentences is by joining the main clauses with a connecting word and a comma. The connecting words to remember are called **coordinating conjunctions.**

Use these short connecting words, with commas before them, to join main clauses:

, and

, but

, or

, nor

, yet

, so

, for

Compare this comma-spliced sentence with the correct one using a comma with a conjunction.

**Comma splice:** The retail price of the dress is *$41.95,* **the** wholesale price is *$25.*

**Correction:** The retail price of the dress is *$41.95,* **but** the wholesale price is *$25.*

Here is an example of a comma-spliced sentence corrected all three ways.

**Comma splice:** Sandra enjoyed hospital serials, she never missed an episode of *Grey's Anatomy.*

**Corrections:** Sandra enjoyed hospital serials. She never missed an episode of *Grey's Anatomy.*

Sandra enjoyed hospital serials; she never missed an episode of *Grey's Anatomy.*

Sandra enjoyed hospital serials, and she never missed an episode of *Grey's Anatomy.*

---

### TEST YOURSELF: Comma Splices

Correct each comma splice by one of three methods: (1) insert a semicolon, (2) divide into two sentences, or (3) add a short connective word. One sentence is correct.

1. The meeting lasted until 4:30, at that point Sonia had to leave.
2. Steve finally went to the dentist, he knew he had at least three cavities.
3. Marsha visited Las Vegas, and she won $100 in a casino.
4. Amy and Ted had a baby girl, they named her Madison.
5. Frank is taking a course online, he thinks he will get an A.
6. The album has nothing new in it, it is becoming popular anyway.
7. Tyrone has been accepted at three colleges, he has to make a choice by Friday.

*Suggested answers:* 1. 4:30. At that point Sonia 2. ; he knew he had 3. correct 4. ; they named her 5. ; he thinks 6. in it, but it is becoming 7. colleges. He has to

## Basic Exercise: Comma Splices

The sentences below were written by students. Correct each comma splice by one of three methods: (1) insert a semicolon, (2) divide into two sentences, or (3) add a short connective word. One sentence is correct.

1. Many people need jobs, therefore better training should be available to help them pursue their careers.
2. My nephew watches violent programs on television all the time, as a result he is starting to adopt loud and violent behavior.
3. Some people believe that teenagers need to know more about managing money, they argue that high schools should teach the subject.
4. Forty years ago parents used to think that it was all right to use physical force to discipline their children, but nowadays that is called child abuse.
5. After that experience I started to enjoy being alone, I discovered a few things about myself.
6. This move to the other office was not by choice, she had to do it.
7. At the party I saw someone I knew, we both went to the same high school.

## Intermediate Exercise: Comma Splices

The sentences below were written by students. Correct each comma splice by one of three methods: (1) insert a semicolon, (2) divide into two sentences, or (3) add a short connective word. One sentence is correct.

1. Hollywood and television celebrities sometimes engage in crazy behavior, their careers almost always benefit from the publicity they receive.
2. Provocative ways of dressing are no longer limited to teenagers, eight- and nine-year-olds are now dressing like their media idols.
3. Adolescents demand more freedom than ever; they nevertheless take longer to grow up and assume adult responsibilities.
4. Obesity has become an intensifying health concern, cases of diabetes and other diseases caused by excessive weight are proliferating.
5. Stores generally offer sales after the holidays, this year the volume of these sales made up for the downturn in holiday buying.

6. The real estate crisis of 2008 caused many people to be wary of buying houses and apartments, nevertheless, many families still dream of owning their own home.

7. Emergency rooms in real hospitals are less frantic than those on television, in fact, patients often wait quietly for hours to receive care.

### Challenge Exercise: Comma Splices

Correct each comma splice below by one of three methods: (1) insert a semicolon, (2) divide into two sentences, or (3) add a short connective word. One sentence is correct.

1. Organic chemistry is required of all premedical students, it often determines whether a student can survive in the program.

2. Some circumstantial evidence can be very persuasive, to be conclusive, however, it must be presented in a logical, understandable way.

3. Cloning human beings was already presented as a future possibility in Woody Allen's 1979 film *Sleeper*, every year it becomes the subject of more heated debate.

4. Bawdy humor did not begin with Hollywood films and stand-up comedians; in fact, Aristophanes in ancient Greece and Rabelais in Renaissance France used it extensively.

5. Departments of media studies have become numerous across the country, they continue to attract large numbers of students interested in careers in broadcast journalism.

6. Thorstein Veblen was a famous sociologist of the early twentieth century, he invented well-known phrases such as "conspicuous consumption."

7. Raising educational standards through instruments of objective assessment is a start toward improving education, however, it is much easier to demand higher test scores than to improve students' achievement.

## Subordinating

A fourth way to correct run-on sentences and comma splices is to **subordinate** one statement to another, creating a complex sentence. This means to turn one of the main clauses into a subordinate clause. Do this by adding one of the subordinate conjunctions like *because* or *when* to one of the main clauses or by beginning one of the main clauses with *who*, *which*, or *that* (making that clause a **relative subordinate clause**).

| **Run-on sentence:** | The students felt nervous they had an examination that morning. |
|---|---|
| **Correction by subordinating one clause:** | The students felt nervous *because* they had an examination that morning. |
| | The students, *who* had an examination that morning, felt nervous. |

## Subordinate Conjunctions: A Short List

Use some of the following words at the beginning of clauses to make them subordinate clauses: *after, although, as, as if, as long as, because, before, even though, if, since, when, whenever, where, whereas, wherever, while.*

---

### TEST YOURSELF: Subordinating

Rewrite these run-on and comma-spliced sentences by subordinating one clause to the other.

1. Everyone in town was excited the home team won the tournament.
2. Beverly is the chairperson of the committee, she wants to change the bylaws.
3. Bob and Frank arrived at noon they looked tired from their trip.
4. Lester is no expert mechanic, he tried to repair his car.
5. The book was long Alison was able to finish it before class.
6. The new hairstyle suited her appearance, Evelyn wanted to try it.
7. You often walk by the supermarket, could you pick up some cereal?

*Answers:* Answers may vary; these are possibilities. 1. excited because 2. Beverly, who is . . . committee, wants 3. When Bob and Frank . . . noon, they 4. Although Lester . . . 5. Even though the book was long, Alison 6. Because the new hairstyle . . . 7. Since you often . . .

---

WRITING EXERCISES: Basic, Intermediate, Challenge

## Basic Exercise: Subordinating

Rewrite these run-on and comma-spliced sentences by subordinating one clause to the other.

1. Both sisters were sad, the family moved to another neighborhood.
2. Geraldo is the manager of the store he thinks he can boss everybody around.
3. Charlene and Isabel entered the gym they were expecting it to be crowded.
4. The editor knows a lot about economics, he often writes articles about social security.
5. The film became boring members of the audience began walking out.
6. The hit single reached the top of the charts, teenagers were not eager to buy it.
7. You can speak Spanish will you please translate the passage?

## Intermediate Exercise: Subordinating

Rewrite these run-on and comma-spliced sentences by subordinating one clause to the other.

1. Immigration has increased in the Southwest, schools have become crowded.
2. The pilot was inexperienced, he didn't know how to navigate in the storm.
3. Several newspapers reported the election results prematurely, confusion resulted.
4. Global warming has been doubted, nearly all scientists are now convinced it is happening.
5. Authors give readings on book tours the sales of their books usually increase.
6. The professor becomes irritated cell phones go off frequently in her class.
7. The members of the band had rehearsed for two hours, they were exhausted.

## Challenge Exercise: Subordinating

Rewrite these run-on and comma-spliced sentences by subordinating one clause to the other.

1. T. S. Eliot was born in St. Louis and educated at Harvard University he became a British citizen in 1927.
2. Einstein proposed the Special Theory of Relativity in 1905, he expanded it to include the General Theory of Relativity in 1916.

3. Many of Sigmund Freud's insights into the psyche are still accepted by psychoanalysts, others have been called into doubt by research on the brain.

4. Osama bin Laden was born in Yemen, he was the only child of his father's tenth wife.

5. On the Indonesian island of Flores scientists discovered the skeleton of a three-foot-tall woman, it was about 18,000 years old and belonged to a homonid that walked upright.

6. The early battles of the Civil War did not go well for the Union army, they created great worry among political and military leaders in the North.

7. Literary theories of various kinds were popular during the 1980s and 1990s, some critics have since returned to more traditional studies such as biographical and formal criticism.

## Key Words from Chapter 7 for Review

comma splice, coordinating conjunction, fragment, relative subordinate clause, subject, run-on sentence, subordinate

# Matching Sentence Parts

---

### STEPPING UP: WRITING TIP 8

Matching subjects and verbs as well as other parts of sentences occurs on different levels. It can be a simple matter of writing *he doesn't* instead of *he don't*. But it often involves longer, more complicated sentences in which you will have to pick out the parts that must be matched properly. Don't expect instinct to guide you in these cases. You might have to pare sentences down to their skeletal structures before you can be sure how to match the parts correctly. To do that requires some knowledge of grammar. But don't be afraid to write just because you are not an expert in grammar. Perfect grammar is an ideal to be aimed for, but very few writers can claim to be grammatically infallible.

---

## Writing Assignments: Noticing Your Sentences

Sometimes the grammar check on your computer may flag one of your sentences and warn you, "Long sentence—no suggestions." That may startle you, especially if you are the kind of writer whose words flow along like conversation with little attention to sentence length and form. What should you do about such "long" sentences? Shorten them? Rewrite them? The first step in sentence mastery is simply paying attention to the sentences you write. Often you will do this *after* you have written a paragraph or essay, as you won't want to stop after every sentence and analyze it, probably losing your train of thought in the process.

Avoid three kinds of sentence patterns: too short, too long, and too repetitious. If you write in nothing but short, simple sentences, your writing will sound immature. If you get lost in loose, endless sentences, your reader will become impatient and lose interest. If you begin every sentence the same way, repeating, for example, the subject–verb–object pattern, your style will be monotonous.

You already have sentence habits; the starting point now is to identify them and see whether they need improvement. Remember that sentences should be varied in length and form. The great writers, of course, create effects with sentence style and rhythm that most of us could not equal, but we can write with our own style and grace by improving our sentence patterns.

In order to recognize your own sentence habits, choose five of the following topics and write a paragraph on each one. Try to stay on topic and express your thoughts and feelings honestly. Then go back and examine your sentences, especially their length and form.

- Tell about a responsibility you chose to accept and explain how well you fulfilled it.
- Tell about an experience you had in a hospital, either an operation you underwent or a series of visits to someone else being treated.
- Imagine yourself in a career or position you would enjoy. Explain what you would do and how you would behave.
- Describe a public figure and explain what you like and dislike about him or her.
- Write a sentence that begins, "I am the person I am today because of. . .". Complete your paragraph by developing the thought stated in that sentence.
- Write a sentence that begins, "What convinced me that I could succeed was. . .". Complete your paragraph by developing the thought stated in that sentence.
- Write a sentence that begins, "The best advice I ever got was. . .". Complete your paragraph by developing the thought stated in that sentence.

Make it a habit to notice sentences in the stories, essays, and articles you read. Pay attention to their length, shape, and rhythm. For practice in noticing sentences, read the following paragraphs and respond to the prompts afterward.

## Model Paragraph: Basic Level

Dwayne's first day at the college presented some unexpected experiences. Although he was ready for something different from high school, he had no idea how much he would have to adjust to college life. First of all, the orientation meeting with other students in his engineering program was a surprise, partly a pleasant one. In high school, all of the students who wanted to become engineers were guys, ones a lot like himself, but here he met women as well as men of different ages who came from Asia, Europe, Africa, and the Middle East. This, he thought, would be an exciting experience, though he worried a little about the competition he would face. Less exciting was the process of registering for courses, since he had to go through four steps and fill out endless forms before he was finished, and he was displeased to find that the courses he most wanted were already filled on the days he preferred. Because this was his first year, however, he assumed the process would become easier. It had been a good start.

1. How many sentences are there in this paragraph? How does this compare with the paragraphs you generally write?
2. Identify two short sentences in this paragraph.
3. Identify the longest sentence in this paragraph. How does it compare in length with the longest sentences you write?
4. Identify at least two sentences that do not begin immediately with the subject.
5. Explain how these sentences begin.
6. Identify a sentence containing a series (list of items in a row) that provides variety.
7. Examine the paragraphs you have just written, and compare your sentences with those in the paragraph above. Do you vary the length and form of your sentences?

# Model Paragraph: Intermediate Level

The great exception to this rule of the recent melting pot is the world's most populous nation, China. Today, China appears politically, culturally, and linguistically monolithic, at least to laypeople. It was already unified politically in 221 B.C. and has remained so for most of the centuries since then. From the beginnings of literacy in China, it has had only a single writing system, whereas modern Europe uses dozens of modified alphabets. Of China's 1.2 billion people, over 800 million speak Mandarin, the language with by far the largest number of native speakers in the world. Some 300 million others speak seven other languages as similar to Mandarin, and to each other, as Spanish is to Italian. Thus, not only is China not a melting pot, but it seems absurd to ask how China became Chinese. China has *been* Chinese, almost from the beginnings of its recorded history.

—Jared Diamond, "How China Became Chinese." *Guns, Germs, and Steel: The Fates of Human Societies* (New York: Norton, 1997), 323.

1. Explain the meaning of *melting pot, monolithic, laypeople,* and *literacy.* What is Mandarin?
2. Describe the sentences in this paragraph: How long are they? Are they similar or different in length and form?
3. Describe the way the sentences begin: Are they all the same, or does the author vary his sentence beginnings?
4. Identify a series (a list of three or more items in a row) used to add variety to one sentence.
5. How many sentences begin with a series of prepositional phrases (phrases using words like *of, in, with,* etc.)?
6. How many sentences begin with introductory connecting words like *hence, however, thus, then, today, usually,* etc.?
7. Copy one of the long sentences in this paragraph and write a sentence of your own, using the same structure.

# Model Paragraph: Challenge Level

Abolitionism was part of a broader struggle for equal justice based on natural rights. Looking back over years of abolitionist activity, William Lloyd Garrison, the fiery editor of the *Boston Liberator*, declared in 1852 that the antislavery movement had begun out of concern for blacks but grew into a crusade for the fundamental liberties of all people. Abolitionists saw slavery as unjust not only because it threatened an entire people with bondage but also because it encouraged the development of a class of aristocratic landowners who had conspired to win power by spreading slavery throughout the Southern states. Furthermore, the abolitionist Wendell Phillips warned, the "slaveocracy" would unite with Northern industrial capitalists to form "the Lords of the Lash and the Lords of the Loom." Garrison called for the immediate emancipation of slaves with no compensation to owners. If the state, church, and American Union could not survive the antislavery movement's call for humanity and freedom, he once exclaimed, they deserved to collapse. "If the Republic must be blotted out from the roll of nations, by proclaiming liberty to the captives, then let the Republic sink beneath the waves of oblivion."

—Howard Jones, *Mutiny on the* Amistad (New York: Oxford University Press, 1987), 8.

1. Define the following words, using a dictionary, if necessary: *abolitionist, crusade, aristocratic, capitalists, emancipation, compensation, oblivion.*
2. Explain the meaning of the following phrases: "equal justice based on natural rights," "crusade for the fundamental liberties of all people," "conspired to win power by spreading slavery," "the Lords of the Lash and the Lords of the Loom."
3. Identify one very short sentence in the paragraph. Where does it occur, and why is it placed where it is?
4. Identify the longest sentence in the paragraph. Explain what phrasing device the author uses to hold it together.
5. Identify a sentence that contains a direct quotation.
6. Identify a sentence that contains an indirect quotation (i.e., it states what the person said but not in his exact words enclosed in quotation marks).
7. Identify at least one parenthetical phrase (a phrase that interrupts the sentence to add an extra comment or identifying fact) used to add variety to the form of the sentence.

## Matching Subjects and Verbs

Every complete sentence contains a subject and verb that go together.

The *band plays* in the stadium.

In this sentence, *band* is the subject, and *plays* is the verb. This sentence is in the present tense, which means you must remember to put the –s ending on *plays*. That is because the subject is **singular:** There is only one band.

In the past tense, you need not worry about whether the subject is singular.

The *band played* in the stadium.
Twelve *bands played* in the stadium.

In the past, the –ed ending will be there no matter what the subject is. In the past tense, then, subject-verb agreement is not a problem—with one exception: the verb forms *was* and *were*.

The *band was* playing in the stadium.
Twelve *bands were* playing in the stadium.

Notice that in this case, the singular *band* takes *was*, and the **plural** (indicating more than one) *bands* takes *were*.

**Subject–verb agreement** boils down to one question: When should you use the –s ending? You might want to look ahead to Verb and Noun Endings in Chapter 9 for a review of the different uses of the –s ending.

Look at the following subject-verb combinations in the present tense.

|  | **Singular** | **Plural** |
|---|---|---|
| **First person** | I succeed | We succeed |
| **Second person** | You succeed | You succeed |
| **Third person** | *She succeeds* | They succeed |

Notice that the underlined combination is in the third person singular. Unlike the others, the verb takes an –s ending. To match your subjects and verbs, you must be able to recognize this one pattern. In all other cases, verbs have no endings in English in the present tense. Compare these examples.

| First person singular: | I enjoy surfing the Web. |
|---|---|
| Third person singular: | She/he enjoys surfing the Web. |
| Third person plural: | They enjoy surfing the Web. |

Most errors in subject-verb agreement involve missing –s endings on nouns or verbs. Either writers put –s endings where they should not be or omit them where they should be.

| Incorrect singular statement: | Tanieka insist on working late. |
|---|---|
| Corrected form: | Tanieka insists on working late. |
| Incorrect plural statement: | Television viewers prefers call-in shows. |
| Corrected form: | Television viewers prefer call-in shows. |

---

**TEST YOURSELF: Correcting Basic Errors in Agreement**

Some of the verbs in the following sentences agree with their subjects; some do not. If the verb is correct, write C in the blank; if not, write the correct form.

1. Cellular phones provides many advantages. _____
2. People who use them like to carry them everywhere. _____
3. Sometimes they interrupts classes and movies. _____
4. Drivers also cause accidents by talking on cell phones. _____
5. People's lives has been saved by cell phones as well. _____
6. The monthly bill for a cell phone often run quite high. _____
7. Special plans, however, offers reduced rates. _____

*Answers:* 1. provide 2. C 3. interrupt 4. C 5. have 6. runs 7. offer

---

**WRITING EXERCISES: Basic, Intermediate, Challenge**

## Basic Exercise: Correcting Errors in Agreement

Underline the subject and circle the correct verb form in each sentence.

1. The street vendor always (stop, stops) me when I walk by.
2. Every morning my stepsister (take, takes) the bus to the campus.
3. Pregnant women (avoid, avoids) using tobacco and alcohol.
4. The Web site (look, looks) more attractive with these improvements.
5. After I study the table of contents, I usually (read, reads) the chapter headings.
6. Most children (like, likes) to play video games.
7. You probably (was, were) the best performer in the show.

## Intermediate Exercise: Correcting Errors in Agreement

Underline the subject and circle the correct verb form in each sentence.

1. Advertisements on television sometimes (interrupt, interrupts) good programs.
2. The last quarter of the game always (prove, proves) to be the most exciting.
3. Most of the money in the fund (belong, belongs) to the retirees.
4. On weekends Sonya and her brother Trevor often (visit, visits) their grandmother.
5. One of the drivers of the van always (insist, insists) on taking a shortcut.
6. Isabel, who always solves customers' problems, (deserve, deserves) a promotion.
7. Sometimes the patient's feelings about the operation (get, gets) lost in the confusion.

## Challenge Exercise: Correcting Errors in Agreement

Underline the subject and circle the correct verb form in each sentence.

1. Calculating the compound interest on accounts sometimes (confuse, confuses) new employees.
2. The mere act of reading without understanding the words (mean, means) very little.
3. Efforts to rescue the people trapped by the earthquake (need, needs) to be made at once.
4. What you do for other people (bring, brings) good deeds in return.
5. On the opposite side of the question there (remain, remains) two weighty arguments.
6. The cost of groceries, rent, and gasoline (keep, keeps) rising.
7. Where you decide to attend college (affect, affects) your future.

# Matching Pronouns and Antecedents

Because **pronouns** take the place of nouns, they always have nouns called **antecedents**, usually in the same sentence or the one just before it, to which they refer. Pronouns must agree with their antecedents in number, person, and gender.

1. **Pronouns and antecedents must agree in number.**
   The *car* lost *its* tailpipe. (*Car* and *its* are both singular.)
   Most *people* enjoy *their* vacations. (*People* and *their* are
   both plural.)
2. **Pronouns and antecedents must agree in person.**
   The *college* changed *its* name. (*College* and *its* are both in the
   third person.)
   *You* should wear *your* hair short. (*You* and *your* are both in the
   second person.)
3. **Pronouns and antecedents must agree in gender.**
   *Sharon* had *her* computer repaired. (*Sharon* and *her* are
   feminine.)
   *John* found *his* sister. (*John* and *his* are masculine.)

Most mistakes in agreement of pronouns and antecedents have
to do with number. Do not shift from a singular noun to a plural
pronoun, or vice versa.

| | |
|---|---|
| **Awkward shifts:** | The *company* changed *their* hiring policy this year. (*Company* is singular; *their* is plural.) |
| | Athletes who use *steroids* often underestimate how harmful *it* is. (*Steroids* is plural; *it* is singular.) |
| **Better:** | The *company* changed *its* hiring policy this year. |
| | Athletes who use *steroids* often underestimate how harmful *they are*. |

**Note:** Indefinite pronouns like *everyone, everybody, anyone, someone,* and *nobody*
are singular. Use singular forms like *he* or *she* to agree with them.

*Anyone* who goes there is putting *his or her* life in danger.

---

**TEST YOURSELF: Matching Pronouns and Antecedents**

Circle the correct pronoun in each sentence.

1. Every woman in the audience knows this is true for (them, her, she).
2. All of the people who voted in the last election expressed (his, her, their) preferences.
3. A law that is not enforced loses (their, his, its) validity.
4. Steps are being taken to prevent looting because (they, it) causes enormous damage.
5. Drugs are an increasing problem among teenagers, and (they, he, it) may cause even worse problems in the next decade.

6. Mothers and fathers have recently pooled (her, his, their) knowledge in writing this book.
7. A firefighter who stays on the force for twenty years receives (his, her, his or her, their) retirement benefits.

*Answers:* 1. her 2. their 3. its 4. it 5. they 6. their 7. his or her

WRITING EXERCISES: Basic, Intermediate, Challenge

# Basic Exercise: Matching Pronouns and Antecedents

Find the incorrect pronouns in these sentences and correct them. One sentence is correct.

1. James and Jeremy decided to leave his job at the same time.
2. A woman in the audience left their handbag on the seat.
3. A man who has taken anger management training won't lose their temper so often.
4. Both cars that she rented had lost its tailpipe.
5. A parent who reads books on child care will raise their children better.
6. The copies that you gave me don't all have their title pages.
7. Both of Denise's jobs were boring, and it was low-paying as well.

# Intermediate Exercise: Matching Pronouns and Antecedents

Find the incorrect pronouns in these sentences and correct them. One sentence is correct.

1. Drugs have created political problems in many countries; it has become a source of crime and corruption.
2. Books that have prices listed on its covers will be sold at a 25 percent discount.
3. The state government is supposed to have their budget ready by April 1.
4. Men who become nurses are aware that he is working in a field once defined as women's work.
5. Special procedures are required for cases involving terrorist threats; trainees must learn it thoroughly.

6. A bystander was reported to have witnessed the accident and left their name with the police.

7. Many politicians promise to lower taxes and provide better services, but not many voters believe them.

### Challenge Exercise: Matching Pronouns and Antecedents

Find the incorrect pronouns in these sentences and correct them. One sentence is correct.

1. The subject of multiple intelligences is taken up in the course, and they are discussed in the third chapter of the textbook as well.

2. Cultural theory, media studies, and gender studies flourished during the 1990s, and it is still popular at many graduate schools.

3. One female biologist specializing in cell research decided to broaden her range of knowledge by earning a second degree in chemistry.

4. Legal interpretation of texts is different from literary interpretation because they require that the reader know the legal meaning of words.

5. Crime rates declined during the last decade in major cities; experts say it fell because of at least three main factors.

6. A student training in a music conservatory today learns to adapt to the realities of the music business which they will face as soon as they graduate.

7. Books about gifted children, also called *child prodigies,* have often stressed the mystique of genius, implying that he gets his usual abilities just from genes and not from hard work.

# Matching Parallel Parts

When you write sentences that contain three or more elements in a series, all elements in the series must belong together; this matching of parts is called **parallelism**.

All elements in a series should be the same **parts of speech**. At this point, you should review briefly the list of parts of speech on page 137. When elements in a series are not parallel, it is because all are nouns, or verbs, or adjectives except one, which is a different part of speech.

Don't try to match parts that don't fit.

| | adj | adj | v |
|---|---|---|---|

**Incorrect:** My neighbor is nosy, competitive, and *likes to pick quarrels.*

Be sure that all elements fit.

| | adj | adj | adj |
|---|---|---|---|

**Correct:** My neighbor is nosy, competitive, and *quarrelsome.*

Or, if one element doesn't fit, take it out and put it in a separate sentence:

**Also Correct:** My neighbor is nosy and competitive. *Besides that, he likes to pick quarrels.*

## TEST YOURSELF: Parallel Parts

Identify the element in each series that does not match the others.

1. Attractive, works hard, and ambitious
2. Into the suburbs, across the bridge, and arrived in the city
3. Expensive to buy, difficult to maintain, and often break down
4. Measuring the room, the windows, mixing the paint, and patching the cracks
5. Of strength, focus, intelligent, and persistence
6. To read, to speak, to listen, and able to understand
7. She drove, he read the map, and in heavy traffic

*Answers:* The elements that don't match are the following: 1. works hard 2. arrived in the city 3. often break down 4. the windows 5. intelligent 6. able to understand 7. in heavy traffic

## WRITING EXERCISES: Basic, Intermediate, Challenge

# Basic Exercise: Parallelism

Rewrite each sentence so that the parallel series is correct. One sentence is correct.

1. Most of my friends are thoughtful, caring, and act in an honest way.
2. The film was exciting, beautiful, and lasted only a short time.

3. Sharon likes to dance, sing, directing films, and cook.
4. Harry walked across the campus, over the bridge, and into the mall.
5. Andrea performed gracefully, spontaneously, and she had a lot of confidence.
6. The team included Naomi, Stacey, and they were joined by Natalie.
7. Leon's goals are to finish his degree, get a better job, and traveling in Mexico.

## Intermediate Exercise: Parallelism

Rewrite each sentence so that the parallel series is correct. If necessary, remove the nonparallel part and add a new statement. One sentence is correct.

1. Computer programming, public speaking, and how to do creative writing are offered by the college.
2. There are several things you should do to stay healthy: get plenty of sleep, exercise regularly, and eating nutritious food.
3. Registering for courses in your first semester takes a lot of persistence, patience, resourcefulness, and you have to be realistic.
4. To get to the theater, take the Number 1 bus to High Street, two blocks to your left, cross the street, and go up the ramp to the right.
5. Sports utility vehicles are popular because they perform well on all kinds of surfaces, hold up under difficult weather conditions, and room for six passengers.
6. The tourists walking on the boardwalk saw bands performing, couples dancing, sunbathers relaxing on the shore, and customers eating in outdoor restaurants.
7. Sarah Palin became well known for being elected governor of Alaska, running for vice president in 2008, and wrote a best-selling book called *Going Rogue: An American Life* in 2009.

## Challenge Exercise: Parallelism

Rewrite each sentence so that the parallel series is correct. If necessary, remove the nonparallel part and add a new sentence. One sentence is correct.

1. The biographers stress many of the former prime minister's strengths: his skill in diplomacy, his leadership in education, his

grasp of economic policy, and praising the way he related to the media.

2. James Thurber's story tells about a man who is dominated by his wife, dreams of being a heroic fighter pilot, and often absent minded, sometimes forgets where he is.

3. The study of philosophy includes metaphysics, aesthetics, learning to be logical, and ethics.

4. To write a research paper correctly, students must use the specialized bibliography format appropriate to each discipline—MLA format for humanities papers, APA format for papers in psychology, and one other well-known format is the CBE style for the sciences and mathematics.

5. Ancient Greece is admired and studied for its philosophical wisdom, its original contributions to scientific knowledge, it set an example as the first real democracy in the world, and its creative literature.

6. Modernism in the arts reflected through experimental style the deeper changes in society, philosophy, world politics, and psychology.

7. New subatomic particles have interesting names such as gluons, hadrons, muons, and there are even quarks, which were named in 1964 by two scientists.

## Key Words from Chapter 8 for Review

antecedent, first person, parallelism, parts of speech, plural, pronoun, second person, singular, subject–verb agreement, third person

# Using Words Correctly

---

## STEPPING UP: WRITING TIP 9

Choosing words well, spelling them correctly, and using their forms correctly can mean the difference between a mediocre paragraph or essay and an outstanding one. Choosing words well requires some care and creativity and the help of a thesaurus. Correct spelling requires you to learn the patterns and exercise care in proofreading. English is a difficult language to spell, even for native speakers, and many words also have endings, primarily –s and –d endings, which can be especially tricky for anyone writing English as a second language. Even native speakers cannot always rely on what sounds right, because many endings are not clearly pronounced in ordinary conversation. Some –d endings, for example, are almost inaudible in conversation (take, for instance, *supposed to* or *used to*—can you hear a /d/ sound in either one?). Reading aloud carefully and slowly, while pronouncing word endings clearly, will help you develop more reliable habits.

---

# Writing Assignment: Noticing Your Use of Words

As you do the exercises in this chapter, look through your own writings to find your strengths as well as your errors in the choice and use of words. You may want to use paragraphs you have already written to provide examples for this purpose. As you work on grammar, however, you should continue doing plenty of new writing. For additional practice, some topics follow. You should learn grammar as part of your own proofreading and editing, not just as a disconnected set of exercises. Apply whatever you learn in these exercises to your own use of words in the paragraphs you compose.

To do more paragraph writing, then, choose five of the following subjects and write a fully developed paragraph on each one. Try to stay on topic and express your thoughts and feelings honestly; remember to include vivid details. Use these paragraphs for noticing your own use of words in the context of paragraph writing.

- Explain what kind of exercise you do, how often, and why. Use details to explain exactly what sort of sports activities or workouts you enjoy.
- Explain how your view of your parents has changed since you were younger. Be specific about what caused your perceptions to change—either changes in your attitude or changes in their behavior.
- Tell about a time when you experienced something you had never done before, such as appearing in court, attending a ceremony in a religion you were unfamiliar with, or spending time with people who spoke a language you didn't know.
- Find a key word that best describes an unusual person in your neighborhood, someone very different from you. Use details to show how the person displays this unusual quality in his or her appearance and actions.
- Describe a place of entertainment that you attend frequently, such as a sports arena, dance venue, movie theater, or concert hall. Use plenty of details to capture the important qualities of this place.
- Compare two places you have visited on vacation. Using details to explain the differences, tell why you enjoyed one vacation spot more than the other.
- Write a persuasive paragraph trying to convince a classmate to join an organization to which you belong. Explain the benefits you

gain from participating and tell why he or she would enjoy the activities offered.

---

## MODEL PARAGRAPHS: Seeing Words in Context

The following paragraphs, written by professional writers, demonstrate particularly effective use of individual words. Follow-up questions will guide you in noticing such matters as diction, range of vocabulary, word forms, capitalization, and spelling. The purpose of this section is to keep your focus on the process of revision and correction in order to improve the effectiveness of your final drafts.

## Model Paragraph: Basic Level

By daylight on Sunday morning my father was placid, the very portrait of composure. Gone were the sweaty work clothes. He had changed into his Sunday best, and the air around him sang with Mennen Speed Stick and Old Spice cologne. He was resplendent in pleated gabardine pants, his dress shoes buffed to a high sheen. His sleeveless summer T-shirt showed off his arms to advantage: He was thin but strong; the muscles moved visibly beneath his skin when he turned the pages of the newspaper or reached for the plate of sliced cantaloupe on the hassock in front of him.

—Brent Staples, *Parallel Time: Growing Up in Black and White*
(New York: Avon Books, 1994), 36.

1. Identify words whose definitions you do not already know and look them up in the dictionary.
2. Find descriptive words (adjectives) that give a specific visual impression.
3. Find action words (verbs) that create the impression of a specific motion or gesture.
4. Identify some words referring to objects (nouns) that give a concrete identity or quality to the objects.
5. Which of the five senses other than vision are brought into the description?
6. How is the fact that it is Sunday morning related to the description of the author's father?
7. In a sentence or two, explain what overall attitude or feeling toward his father the author conveys to you in this paragraph.

# Model Paragraph: Intermediate Level

One afternoon the twins made a thrilling find, spotting the tail rotor of a helicopter that had crashed behind a bombed-out farmhouse. It had been there for at least a week, to judge from the remains of the pilots scattered about the wreck, the birds and rodents and feral dogs having worked to leave them almost cleanly skeletal inside the torn uniforms. Broken beer bottles littered the floor of the cockpit. But in a crate behind the seats there was a hold of pristine riches: a half-dozen packets of beef jerky and a can of Spam. As with the tins June found, they couldn't help but eat the canned meat right away; their mother refused it, professing not to like its smell as she cut the pinkish block into four thick slices with the edge of the can, though while she was gorging on the salty, slick meat June saw her mother take a taste of her fingertips, her eyes half shut, losing herself for a moment in another time and place.

—Chang-Rae Lee, *The Surrendered*
(New York: Riverhead Books, 2010), 18.

1. The scene being described is set in a time of war. Identify details that reveal the wartime setting.
2. Define the following words; use a dictionary, if necessary: *feral*, *pristine*, *jerky*, *gorging*.
3. Identify words (nouns) that name specific objects.
4. Identify words (verbs) that convey specific actions.
5. Identify modifying words (adjectives and adverbs) that capture the quality of the experience.
6. Explain what feelings the author's description creates in the reader.
7. Identify words that appeal to the senses of vision, feeling, and taste.

# Model Paragraph: Challenge Level

The starting point for acknowledging human nature is a sheer awe and humility in the face of the staggering complexity of its source, the brain. Organized by the three billion bases of our genome and shaped by hundreds of millions of years of evolution, the brain is a network of unimaginable intricacy: a hundred billion neurons linked by a hundred trillion connections, woven into a convoluted three-dimensional architecture.

Humbling, too, is the complexity of what it does. Even the mundane talents we share with other primates—walking, grasping, recognizing—are solutions to engineering problems at or beyond the cutting edge of artificial intelligence. The talents that are human birthrights—speaking and understanding, using common sense, teaching children, inferring other people's motives—will probably not be duplicated by machines in our lifetime, if ever. All this should serve as a counterweight to the image of the mind as formless raw material and to people as insignificant atoms making up the complex being we call "society."

— Steven Pinker, *The Blank Slate* (New York: Viking, 2002), 197.

1. Define the following words; use a dictionary, if necessary: *genome, neurons, convoluted, mundane, primates, inferring*.
2. Explain how the descriptive words *sheer* and *staggering* in the first sentence and *unimaginable* in the second sentence affect the meaning of the words they modify.
3. Explain the meaning of the phrase, *the cutting edge of artificial intelligence*.
4. Why does the author call walking, grasping, and recognizing "mundane talents"?
5. Why does he call speaking, etc., "human birthrights"?
6. In your own words, explain what the author is saying about the brain.
7. Describe the author's attitude toward the human brain.

# Parts of Speech: Seeing How Words Work

In this book we avoid using difficult terms whenever possible. However, it will be a big help if you review the basic categories of word use. We can label all words according to the way we use them in sentences. The eight labels we use are called the **parts of speech.** They include **nouns, pronouns, verbs, adjectives, adverbs, prepositions, conjunctions,** and **interjections.** We call them *parts of speech* rather than *types of words* because a single word can sometimes be used in two ways or more. Is the word *walk* a verb or a noun? If you *walk* to class, it's a verb; if you take a *walk*, it's a noun. When you look up a new word in the dictionary, notice carefully how each definition tells you what part or parts of speech the word can be. Look for abbreviations like *n.* for noun, *adj.* for adjective, etc.

Because we often need to use these labels when talking about grammar, you should study the list below and familiarize yourself with any of these terms you do not already know. Above all, learn to recognize nouns and verbs, which are the main building blocks of sentences.

■ **NOUNS** refer to persons, objects, places, or ideas.

Nouns come in two categories, common nouns and proper nouns. **Common nouns** are *general* words for persons, objects, places, or ideas: *student, beeper, corner, advantage.* Do not capitalize common nouns. **Proper nouns** are *specific* names of individual persons, objects, places, companies, institutions, or other groups: *Justin Bieber, Elton John, Mexico City, Microsoft, Chicago, Afghanistan.* Always capitalize proper nouns.

Nouns also take two forms, singular and plural. **Singular** nouns refer to one person, object, place, or idea: *a student, a beeper, the corner, an advantage.* (If English is not your first language, don't forget to write the article *a, an,* or *the* before singular nouns.) **Plural** nouns refer to two or more persons, objects, places, or ideas: *students, beepers, corners, advantages.* (Don't forget that most plural nouns take *–s* endings.

■ **PRONOUNS** take the place of nouns.

Pronouns come in five categories: personal pronouns, indefinite pronouns, relative pronouns, interrogative pronouns, and demonstrative pronouns.

**Personal pronouns** include all forms of *I, we, you, she, he, they,* and *it,* as well as the reflexive pronouns *myself, ourselves, yourself, yourselves, himself, herself, themselves,* and *itself.* (Remember not to write *theirself, theirselves,* or *hisself.*)

**Indefinite pronouns** are words that refer to a number of persons or things, like *everyone, something, all, many,* and *each.*

**Relative pronouns** introduce clauses that relate to or modify other parts of a sentence. These pronouns include the forms of *who,* as well as *which* and *that.*

**Interrogative pronouns,** used to begin questions, include *who, which,* and *what.*

**Demonstrative pronouns** point out persons, places, or things; they include *this, that, these,* and *those.*

■ **VERBS** designate action or state of being.

**Action verbs** include words like *swim, drive, dance,* and *write.*
**State-of-being verbs** include *be* (in all its forms—*is, was, were,* etc.), *seem, become,* and similar words.

Verbs can take different forms, depending on number and tense. Exercises on verb forms later in this unit will help you learn how to use the correct verb forms and verb endings. The two biggest problems with verbs are using *–s* endings in the present tense and *–d* endings in the past.

■ **ADJECTIVES** describe or modify nouns.

Some adjectives, like *green, prodigious, beautiful,* and *happy,* tell what kind of person or thing is being described. Others, like *twenty, few,* and *innumerable,* tell how many persons or things are being described. And a few adjectives, like *this, that, these,* and *those* (which can also be pronouns when they stand alone), identify which person or thing is being described. Adjectives can take comparative and superlative forms in comparative statements. See the section on modifiers in Chapter 12.

■ **ADVERBS** describe verbs, adjectives, or other adverbs.

Adverbs can designate how, when, or where an action occurs. Many adverbs, like *quickly, permanently,* and *happily,* are formed by adding *–ly* endings to adjectives. Like adjectives, adverbs can take comparative and superlative forms. See the section on modifiers in Chapter 12.

■ **PREPOSITIONS** are the little words or word combinations that show relationship or direction. Prepositions include words like *in, of, on, above, beneath,* and *through,* as well as combinations like *by means of, on behalf of,* and *in regard to.* **Prepositional phrases**, such as *of the students, in the film,* or *with an attitude,* contain prepositions and their objects (the nouns or pronouns that come after them). Identifying prepositional phrases will help you recognize the grammatical structure of sentences. See the section on subject–verb agreement in Chapter 8.

■ **CONJUNCTIONS** are the connecting words that link words, phrases, or whole clauses.

**Coordinating conjunctions** (*and, or, nor, but, yet, so,* and *for*) join equal parts, such as two words (bread *and* butter), two phrases (above the ankles *but* below the knees), or two clauses (she wanted to apply for the job, *yet* she had doubts about it). Coordinating conjunctions are used to join parts of a compound sentence. See the section on run-on sentences in Chapter 7.

**Correlative conjunctions** such as *either/or, not only/but also,* and *both/and,* are used in combination to join words, phrases, or whole clauses. See the section on subject–verb agreement in Chapter 8.

**Subordinating conjunctions,** such as *because, when, if, although,* and *since,* connect main clauses with dependent clauses in complex sentences. See the sections on fragments and run-on sentences in Chapter 7.

■ **INTERJECTIONS** are short words like *oh, well, yes,* and *sure,* and phrases like *Good heavens!* or *Good grief!* that are put at the beginnings of sentences to express strong feeling or surprise. Put commas or exclamation points after them.

---

## TEST YOURSELF: Identifying Parts of Speech

Name the part of speech (noun, pronoun, verb, adjective, adverb, preposition, conjunction, interjection) of each italicized word in the sentences that follow.

1. The *fans* in the *back* row *hooted* loudly and *angrily* during the whole *second* quarter.
2. Most clothing *stores* have *sales* after the holidays *and* occasionally *at* other times.
3. *Popular* music *includes* many *categories*, such as country *music*, heavy metal, *soft* rock, rap, and hip-hop.
4. *When* children *watch* too much television, *they* don't *spend* enough time *on* their homework.
5. *Yes*, the person *who* sent the e-mail *messages* wanted to frighten *or* amuse *members* of the group.
6. Original *ideas* often come *to* us *while* we are thinking about *something* else.
7. *Global* markets *and* foreign *currencies* usually *affect* the economic *policies* of smaller countries.

*Answers:* 1. *fans* (noun), *back* (adjective), *hooted* (verb), *angrily* (adverb), *second* (adjective) 2. *stores* (noun), *sales* (noun), *and* (conjunction), *at* (preposition) 3. *popular* (adjective), *includes* (verb), *categories* (noun), *music* (noun), *soft* (adjective) 4. *when* (conjunction), *watch* (verb), *they* (pronoun), *spend* (verb), *on* (preposition) 5. *yes* (interjection), *who* (pronoun), *messages* (noun), *or* (conjunction), *members* (noun) 6. *ideas* (noun), *to* (preposition), *while* (conjunction), *something* (pronoun) 7. *global* (adjective), *and* (conjunction), *currencies* (noun), *affect* (verb), *policies* (noun)

## Basic Exercise: Parts of Speech

Identify the part of speech of each italicized word in the sentences that follow.

1. The *green* paint *was* still *wet* when *she* touched it.
2. Jeremy *and* Sophia *usually* work *in* the afternoon.
3. *Yes,* my *cousin* still *works* in a bank.
4. *Older* students often *write* long essays.
5. The list *contained* seven *names* of her *best* friends.
6. Boston and *Detroit* *have* many baseball *fans*.
7. *We* took the *shortest* route and drove *rapidly*.

## Intermediate Exercise: Parts of Speech

Identify the parts of speech of each italicized word in the sentences that follow.

1. *Four* candidates *debated* the *issues* on a network broadcast.
2. Veronica spent most of her *spare* time on sports *and* theater.
3. *International* students *organized* a new *club*.
4. The fear of *terrorism* has resulted *in* tighter security *measures*.
5. *Physical* exercise *unquestionably* tends to prolong *life*.
6. *Yes,* the best answer to the *second* question is *obvious*.
7. The *college* raised tuition to pay *for* a *new* stadium.

## Challenge Exercise: Parts of Speech

Identify the parts of speech of each italicized word in the sentences that follow.

1. *Although* many *mental* disorders *are described* in the textbook, few treatments are mentioned.
2. The *influence* of *sociological* research *on* public policies has *often* been noticed.
3. *Neither* computer science *nor* *mathematics* is offered *to first* year students.
4. *When* governments *experience* economic *crises, they* sometimes *appeal* to their *allies* for help.
5. *Contemporary* artists *typically* experiment with *innovative* styles *and* forms.

6. The *study* of philosophy *requires* a *discerning* mind and *lively* imagination.

7. *No*, studying *grammar* will not make you a great *writer*, *but* it will help *you* understand how language *works*.

---

**EXERCISE USING YOUR OWN WRITING:** Identifying the Words You Write

Select the best paragraph that you have written in your journal so far and do the following.

|  verb | noun | adjective | noun |
|---|---|---|---|

*Find* at least one *example* of each of the *eight* parts of *speech* in one

| noun | verb | noun | preposition |
|---|---|---|---|

of your *paragraphs*, and *write* the *label* identifying it *above* the word,

| noun | verb | adverb | noun | conjunction |
|---|---|---|---|---|

as in this *sentence*. *Identify carefully* at least five *nouns and* five verbs.

| interjection | verb | pronoun | verb |
|---|---|---|---|

*Oh*, and please *notice* whether *they have* endings attached to them.

# Verb and Noun Endings

## Adding –s Endings to Words

Many writers have trouble with –s endings. This happens because –*s* endings can be added to words for different reasons. Some words, of course, already end in *s*, like *kiss* or *class*. There are four –*s* endings that we *add* to words:

A. Add –*s* or –*es* to verbs in the third-person singular, present tense: The student *writes*.

B. Add –*s* or –*es* to plural nouns: The *students* write.

C. Add –*'s* to singular possessives: the *student's* essay.

D. Add –*s'* to most plural possessives: four *students'* essays.

(Exception: Add –*'s* to plural possessives when the plural does not already end in –*s*: *women's* opinions.)

## TEST YOURSELF: –s Endings

Using the A, B, C, D categories on the previous page, identify all of these underlined –s endings:

1. Most immigrant<u>s</u> work to meet their familie<u>s</u>' needs.
2. A child who attend<u>s</u> a good school has advantage<u>s</u>.
3. An umpire'<u>s</u> judgment is better than a spectator'<u>s</u>.
4. The student government insist<u>s</u> on fair election<u>s</u>.
5. My neighborhood lack<u>s</u> a men'<u>s</u> clothing store.
6. The correct answer<u>s</u> appear in tomorrow'<u>s</u> edition.
7. Susan'<u>s</u> brother know<u>s</u> you.

*Answers:*1. B, D 2. A, B 3. C, C 4. A, B 5. A, D 6. B, C 7. C, A

---

## WRITING EXERCISES: Basic, Intermediate, Challenge

# Basic Exercise: Identifying –s Endings

Identify each underlined –s ending with one of the following letters: A (singular verb, third person), B (plural noun), C (singular possessive), D (plural possessive).

1. Thomas often give<u>s</u> money to charitie<u>s</u>.
2. Stephanie disagree<u>s</u> with her sister'<u>s</u> opinion<u>s</u> about men.
3. Both employees'<u></u> pay stub<u>s</u> were missing.
4. The interviewer<u>s</u> asked all applicant<u>s</u> the same questions.
5. The bank'<u>s</u> customer<u>s</u> can read their statement<u>s</u> online.
6. Jeremy write<u>s</u> e-mail letter<u>s</u> to his girlfriend.
7. Patricia agree<u>s</u> with her parents'<u></u> values.

# Intermediate Exercise: Identifying –s Endings

Identify each underlined –s ending with one of the following letters: A (singular verb, third person), B (plural noun), C (singular possessive), D (plural possessive).

1. Keats'<u>s</u> poetry is beautiful, especially his ode<u>s</u>.
2. One of the doctor<u>s</u> actually make<u>s</u> house calls during weekend<u>s</u>.
3. Biology 101 carrie<u>s</u> four credit<u>s</u> and is required in most students'<u></u> programs.

4. The football coach's car is the most impressive of all the vehicles in the lot.
5. After changing its sales strategies, the children's clothing store remained in business.
6. The admissions office looks at a student's high school record as well as test scores.
7. Ira is trying to follow both counselors' recommendations, but he finds it difficult.

## Challenge Exercise: Identifying –s Endings

Identify each underlined –s ending with one of the following letters: A (singular verb, third person), B (plural noun), C (singular possessive), D (plural possessive).

1. Critics' reviews, especially in the first weeks, tended to emphasize the film's authenticity.
2. Specialists in children's literature approve of the way the book encourages self-esteem in adolescents.
3. The manager, who always insists that employees comply with elderly customers' requests, received an award.
4. Sharon's running in the marathon was no harder than Sylvia's performing in three ballets.
5. The corrections and erasures that Michael makes on his assignments indicate that he proofreads carefully.
6. One of the scientists' theories still remains to be confirmed by experts' opinions.
7. Whenever the plane's tail vibrates, the passengers' anxiety increases.

---

**WRITING EXERCISES:** Basic, Intermediate, Challenge

## Basic Exercise: Adding –s Endings

Each sentence below has two words with –s endings missing. In the blanks provided, write the two words correctly with their –s endings. Some may require –'s or –s' endings.

1. Hector like to read book
   about history.                    _____    _____
2. Amy prefer story about
   famous women.                     _____    _____

3. The song on Nicole new
album are wonderful.     _____     _____

4. Parent attitude about dating
have changed.     _____     _____

5. There are many way to make
new friend.     _____     _____

6. Jamal job require a college
degree.     _____     _____

7. Isabel call both cousin
every week.     _____     _____

## Intermediate exercise: Adding –s Endings

Each sentence below has either one or two –s endings missing. Find the word or words and add the –s endings. Some may require –'s or –s' endings.

1. Team that win championship do not always have the most money.
2. A political candidate who use the Internet can influence public opinion.
3. Hurricane have devastated many country over the last decade.
4. Declines in the stock market usually reduce worker pension.
5. An athlete who train without using performance-enhancing substance doesn't fear drug testing.
6. State that frequently impose the death penalty still have high murder rate.
7. Having television camera in a courtroom can influence a judge method of conducting a trial.

## Challenge Exercise: Adding –s Endings

Each sentence below has one, two, or three words with –s endings missing. Find the word or words and add –s endings. Some may require –'s or –s' endings.

1. Regular meter and rhyme are two element found in poetry, but not all poet use them.
2. The first two chapter in the textbook define and describe many common psychological disorder.
3. Medical expert repeated warning about the many health hazard of smoking have affected public policy.

4. Dispute resolution require critical thinking, patience, and firmness.
5. Linguistics is the study of the world language, several thousand of which still exist.
6. Changes in a country climate over many decade is bound to affect its economic growth.
7. Modernism was an artistic and literary movement that reflected change in people value.

# Possessives: A Quick Review

You may have been a little uncertain about –s endings in the C and D categories, that is, singular and plural **possessives,** words that show ownership. Don't be too worried: Most people get mixed up about possessives sometimes, especially when the basic rule doesn't fit.

## The Basic Pattern

To show possession with a singular noun, add an apostrophe followed by an s:

one customer's account

If the noun is plural, add an apostrophe after the s:

many customers' accounts

Simple, isn't it? Yes, but what makes possessives confusing is that some singular words already end in –s and some plural words do not. How do you make a possessive out of *Mr. Jones* or *women?* In addition to the basic pattern, you should be familiar with the occasional exceptions.

## The Exceptions

Some singular nouns, especially proper names, already end in –s. In such cases, add an apostrophe without the s (with short, one-syllable names, 's is also acceptable):

Ms. Andrews' office
Dylan Thomas' poems
Keats' odes or Keats's (a one-syllable noun)

Some plural nouns do not end in –s. Instead, they change their spelling to indicate the plural, for example *woman, women; child, children; man, men; mouse, mice.* In such cases, add *'s.*

children's clothing
men's opinions

## TEST YOURSELF: Possessives

Find the word in each sentence that should be in possessive form and write it with the correct ending. If the word is already possessive, write *Correct* in the blank.

_____ 1. Steve thought he understood the teacher instructions.

_____ 2. Barbara plans had to be changed.

_____ 3. Most of the players uniforms are new.

_____ 4. Four of Nicole's poems were in the collection.

_____ 5. Roger subscribed to two men magazines.

_____ 6. On Jonas birthday, his friends gave him a surprise party.

_____ 7. The workshop was about parents responsibilities.

*Answers:* 1. teacher's 2. Barbara's 3. players' 4. correct 5. men's 6. Jonas' 7. parents'

WRITING EXERCISES: Basic, Intermediate, Challenge

# Basic Exercise: Possessives

Identify the possessive form in each sentence and write it correctly. One sentence is correct as is.

1. Elizabeth ambition is to write a screen play.
2. My mother attitudes are surprisingly modern.
3. Teenagers peer groups influence their behavior.
4. Most of Stanley friends are from his school.
5. Men fashions changed this year.
6. Four students' essays were sent by e-mail.
7. Jennifer sister met her at the mall.

# Intermediate Exercise: Possessives

Identify the possessive form in each sentence and write it correctly. One sentence is correct as is.

1. Professor Hughes class meets on Mondays and Wednesdays.
2. My term paper is on Emily Dickinson's poetry.

3. The bank makes customers accounts available online.

4. Some young adults do not listen to their parent advice.

5. The nation economy began improving at the beginning of the year.

6. The talk show host responded to viewers questions.

7. When Alice job schedule changed, she had to drop the course.

## Challenge Exercise: Possessives

Identify the one or two errors in possessive forms in each sentence and write them correctly. One sentence is correct as is.

1. Astronomy and biology are the science department most popular courses.

2. Many psychological factors can influence an authors or an artists work.

3. According to most experts opinions, many company profits will be affected by oil prices.

4. Many Americans admire Ansel Adams photographs of Yosemite National Park.

5. The children literature class discussed J. K. Rowling's books.

6. Some womens studies programs include courses on health and medicine.

7. After her lecture on President Johnson life, the author answered questions.

REVIEW EXERCISES: –s Endings

## Basic Exercise: –s Endings

In the paragraph that follows, find the seven errors in –s endings. They may be words with –s endings missing or words that have incorrect endings. Don't forget to look for possessives as well as plural nouns and singular verbs.

My cousin Samantha think she is smarter than everybody else. Most of Samantha friends are just average student, but she has a 4.00 grade point average. Since she has studied accounting and finance, she also know how to manage money better than other people, so she gives financial advices to her two older brother. She is sure that her parents will be proud of her when she completes her degree, but sometimes she allow her superiority to go to her head.

## Intermediate Exercise: –s Endings

In the paragraph below find the seven errors in –s endings. They may be words with –s endings missing or words that have incorrect endings. Don't forget to look for possessives as well as plural nouns and singular verbs.

Many people decide how to vote by watching candidates on television. Above all, they concentrate on their appearance. They notice the candidate hair, clothes, and jewelry, paying more attention to the way they look and dress than to their political view. When political debates occur, they often seems more like tryouts for film role than serious arguments about important issues. The public becomes aware of a candidate positions only if he or she make a foolish mistake or comes up with a quotable one-line zinger. Some experts believes that voters would do better to study the Web sites about all the candidates than to watch the debates.

## Challenge Exercise: –s Endings

In the paragraph below find the seven errors in –s endings. They may be words with –s endings missing or words that have incorrect endings. Don't forget to look for possessives as well as plural nouns and singular verbs.

Mental disorders that once could be analyzed and treated only through various form of talk therapy are now being treated through a combination of drugs and therapy. Although psychiatrist opinions still differ on which drugs are best for certain disorder, nearly all mental health professional make extensive use of prescription drugs in treating patient who do not respond as quickly to talk therapy alone. Although the prices of some drugs have risen considerably, a patient finances are less likely to be strained by the use of drugs than by lengthy therapy, and the combination of drugs and therapy usually alleviate the problem more quickly than either method by itself.

# Recognizing Tenses

To use correct verb tenses and avoid awkward shifts in tense, you must know the verb tenses and what they mean. There are three basic verb **tenses:** present, past, and future.

| Present: | Jeremy *excels* at film editing. |
| Past: | Jeremy *excelled* at film editing. |
| Future: | Jeremy *will excel* at film editing. |

## Present Tense

In the **present tense**, all verbs take –*s* endings (singular, third person) or no endings (plural and first- and second-person singular).

|  | **Singular** | **Plural** |
| --- | --- | --- |
| First person: | I succeed | We succeed |
| Second person: | You succeed | You succeed |
| Third person: | He, she, it succeeds | They succeed |

## Past Tense

In the **past tense**, verbs fall into two categories: **regular verbs**, which take –*d* endings, and **irregular verbs**, which change their spelling and do not take –*d* endings.

| **Past Tense for Regular Verbs** | **Past Tense for Irregular Verbs** |
| --- | --- |
| accepted | broke |
| expected | brought |
| kissed | came |
| murdered | drank |
| succeeded | drove |
| violated | knew |
| wandered | sang |
| worked | sent |
| worshiped | took |

## Future Tense

All verbs form the **future tense** by adding the helping verb *will* to the main verb with no ending.

| | |
| --- | --- |
| *will* succeed | *will* study |
| *will* deliver | *will* purchase |
| *will* work | *will* spend |
| *will* register | *will* jog |

## TEST YOURSELF: Recognizing Tenses

Determine whether each sentence is written in the past, present, or future tense.

1. Stephanie likes to play the guitar, the flute, and the recorder.
2. We relied on the GPS to help us find our way to the racetrack.
3. The last episode of the series was shot in Hawaii.
4. Another payment will be due on April 1.
5. Some of the spectators who sat in the back row couldn't hear the announcement.
6. Miriam usually sends e-cards to her family on holidays.
7. The weather will be warmer but cloudy over the weekend.

*Answers:*1. present 2. past 3. past 4. future 5. past 6. present 7. future

---

## WRITING EXERCISES: Basic, Intermediate, Challenge

# Basic Exercise: Recognizing Tenses

Identify the tense used in each sentence that follows: past, present, or future.

1. Marisol will be twenty-three years old in March.
2. Jennifer and Vicente entered college at the same time.
3. All students received instructions by e-mail.
4. Tiffany always likes to sit in the front row.
5. Dwayne noticed three of his friends leaving the gym.
6. The boat will leave at three o'clock.
7. Every student in the class writes a research paper.

# Intermediate Exercise: Recognizing Tenses

Identify the tense used in each sentence that follows: past, present, or future.

1. The critics all agreed that it was the best children's film of the year.
2. According to economists, next year will be a good one for the computer industry.
3. Performers who earn most of their income in live performances don't worry about the sales of CDs.
4. Celebrity court cases occupied a large fraction of television news time last year.
5. An adult student often faces the challenge of working, studying, and raising a family at the same time.

6. A liberal arts graduate will sometimes earn less than those with technical training but will have knowledge and skills that will prove valuable in the long run.

7. Changes that occurred in campaign finance laws gave an advantage to rich candidates.

## Challenge Exercise: Recognizing Tenses

Identify the tense used in each sentence that follows: past, present, or future.

1. The main character in Kate Chopin's short story "The Story of an Hour" undergoes a shock when she hears of the death of her husband but soon experiences a psychological transformation.

2. Sigmund Freud's theories and methods of psychoanalysis astonished the experts of his generation but established his name as the father of modern psychoanalysis.

3. The English language will continue to change, acquiring new vocabulary and idioms, and the rules of grammar will no doubt adapt gradually to these changes.

4. The decade of the 1960s combined the Civil Rights Movement, the Women's Movement, the protests against the war in Vietnam, and the demands of students for changes in university policies.

5. The protagonists in both films struggle against daunting obstacles, including not only their families' lack of understanding but also their own fears and inhibitions.

6. The actors who won Academy Awards for Best Actor almost never achieved the Oscar until they had made a number of films and attracted name recognition.

7. The study of physics is far more complicated than in the past, since it includes a new world of subatomic particles and theories of multidimensional universes.

# Verb Tenses and –d Endings

Verb tenses are signaled in several ways in English. We have already studied –s endings:

The –s ending indicates present tense (in the third-person singular only): Jessica enjoys *South Park*.

The −d ending indicates past tense (except for the irregular verbs like *ran* and *went* that change their spelling in the past): Jessica enjo*yed* last night's episode of *South Park*.

## −d Endings in the Past Tense

Do you sometimes drop or forget to add −d endings on regular verbs? Be careful to edit for −d endings when writing in the past tense. At the same time, remember:

## When Not to Use −d Endings

If you tend to omit −d endings in the past tense, remember that there are a few places where −d endings should *not* be used.

1. **After the helping word *did*.** *Did* is already in the past tense and does not need another past tense form to go with it:
   *Did* you *discuss* (not *discussed*) the salary?
   It really *did happen* (not *happened*) that way.
2. **After other helping verbs** (**except** *be* and *have*): *may, might, can, could, will, would, must,* and *should*:
   We *will walk* (not *walked*) there together.
   He *could learn* (not *learned*) a lot from you.
3. **After the word *to*.** A verb with the word *to* in front of it is called an **infinitive**; it is not in the past tense and does not take a −d ending:
   We used *to live* (not *to lived*) in Cincinnati.
   They tried *to reach* (not *to reached*) the turnoff.

---

### TEST YOURSELF: −*d* Endings in the Past Tense

Change the verbs in these sentences to the past tense using −*d* endings.

1. The economics course attracts many students.
2. Valerie designs theater sets for the civic theater.
3. Directing a film excites Sonya as much as acting in it.
4. Something peculiar occurs every time she introduces herself.
5. Passengers suspect terrorism whenever they notice odd behavior.
6. New information forces economists to reconsider their predictions.
7. Some remarkably low prices in the Web auction interest customers.

*Answers:*1. attracted 2. designed 3. excited 4. occurred, introduced 5. suspected, noticed 6. forced 7. interested

---

## Basic Exercise: –*d* Endings

Identify one word in each sentence that has a missing –*d* ending or that should have a –*d* ending removed. One sentence is correct.

1. Roberta place the book on the counter.
2. The suspect was not name in the article.
3. After the argument, James could not faced his brother.
4. Michael admitted that he was already marry.
5. The boss fire three of his employees.
6. Susan was concerned about her test scores.
7. The performance was suppose to be short.

## Intermediate Exercise: –*d* Endings

Identify two words in each sentence that have missing –*d* endings or that should have –*d* endings removed. One sentence is correct.

1. Last semester the college change its admissions requirements and close two programs.
2. The mayor propose new rules about smoking but didn't implemented them yet.
3. Yesterday, the city council pass up a chance to improved the quality of child care.
4. On the first day, the professor mention that she want us to write a journal.
5. The heat of the room cause many students to feel sleepy, and some doze off.
6. Newspapers reported the incident last May, but they didn't include all the details.
7. The couple got marry in April and travel to the Bahamas for their honeymoon.

## Challenge Exercise: –*d* Endings

Find words in these sentences that have –*d* endings missing or that have –*d* endings that should be removed. Each sentence may have one, two, or three errors—or none at all.

1. Raymond Carver, the renown American short story writer, die in 1988 at the age of forty-nine.
2. He live in Port Angeles, Washington, most of his life but also join the faculty at several universities elsewhere.
3. His stories have move readers, impress critics, and influence other writers.
4. He didn't composed novels because his personal life interfere too much with his work.
5. Carver suffer from alcoholism and continue to smoked most of his life.
6. He was marry twice and had two children; he was able to used many of his personal experiences in his fiction.
7. A film called *Short Cuts*, based on several of his stories, was set in Los Angeles but retained some of his plots and characters.

## Key Words from Chapter 9 for Review

adjective, adverb, conjunction (coordinating, correlative, subordinating), infinitive, interjection, noun (common, proper), parts of speech, plural, preposition, prepositional phrase, pronoun (demonstrative, interrogative, indefinite, personal, relative), possessive, singular, tense (past, present, future), verb (action, state-of-being; irregular, regular)

# From Paragraph to Essay

# Building Essays Out of Paragraphs

---

### STEPPING UP: WRITING TIP 10

Some people think it is too mechanical and boring to talk about thesis statements, topic sentences, outlines, and so on. They may argue that such talk will stifle your creativity. You will probably find, however, that having a strong thesis and logical outline will give you the confidence to be original. You may be more creative if you begin with focused writing in which you explore the topic without planning. When you are planning the final essay, however, a lack of direction is likely to block your inspiration; planning and clear thinking will tend to release it.

---

## Starting with a Thesis

When you write an essay, your first and most important question should be, "What is my thesis?" A **thesis** is a lot like the topic sentence in a paragraph, except that it states the overall purpose of your essay. The **topic sentences** of your paragraphs should make specific points that back up the general argument stated in your thesis. To understand the difference between your thesis statement and the topic sentences of your paragraphs, picture yourself as a lawyer defending a client in court.

| | |
|---|---|
| **Thesis Sentence:** | My client is not guilty of murder. |
| **Topic Sentence #1:** | He has an alibi: He was somewhere else at the time. |
| **Topic Sentence #2:** | The circumstantial evidence clearly points to someone else. |
| **Topic Sentence #3:** | He had no motive. |
| **Topic Sentence #4:** | He is not the kind of person who would ever hurt anyone. |

None of these topic sentences would make a whole case by itself, but the defense attorney will construct her case by using all of them together. At the beginning and end of the presentation, the attorney would have to stress her thesis: that the jury should find her client not guilty. Your essay should be like that: It should have a strong purpose that you state near the beginning, reaffirm at the end, and support with topic sentences and plenty of evidence in your middle paragraphs.

## What Makes an Effective Thesis?

Ask yourself—or better, explain to a classmate—what you are trying to prove in the essay. You should be able to do this in a single sentence beginning, "In this essay I argue that (or demonstrate that). . .". In most academic essays, you should make this purpose clear in a **thesis statement** somewhere in your first paragraph. Many writers choose to place their thesis statement near or at the end of their first paragraph. In narrative, descriptive, and other kinds of essays, there may or may not be a single thesis statement, but you should always be able to sum up your purpose in a sentence. In addition, this purpose should come across strongly to your reader.

While being broad enough to require a whole essay of explanation, your thesis should also be sharply defined and meaningful enough to offer the reader something to think about. If it is too limited, you won't be able to write a whole essay supporting it without becoming repetitive. If it is too broad, on the other hand, you may be unable to support and develop it thoroughly. If it is vague, you probably won't say anything original and interesting. Your goal is to find a clearly focused thesis that you can express in a single thesis statement. Notice the difference in the statements that follow.

| Inadequate, Narrow Thesis Statement: | Women are called bad names in hip-hop. |
| --- | --- |
| Broad, Vague Thesis Statement: | Images of women in America are too negative. |
| Focused Thesis Statement: | Images of women in hip-hop music have a negative effect on children's behavior. |

The first sentence above is mostly a factual statement that does not take a position. The statement does not tell the reader what the author is arguing. The second is so all-inclusive that it sounds like the subject of a whole book. The third one might make the subject of a lively essay with a controversial point if the writer knows something about hip-hop music. We can see where it leads and what kind of evidence is needed to support it. While this statement would not guarantee a perfect essay, it would point the writer and the reader in the right direction.

## Introductory Paragraphs

Be sure to do one thing in your **introductory paragraph:** Focus your reader's interest on your thesis. Merely capturing the reader's interest is not enough if you don't aim that interest in the right direction, and merely stating your thesis without making it interesting is a show-stopper. You may want to begin with a short, interesting statement, a question, a paradox, or even a quotation. Then you should make a link to the purpose of your essay, which you state in your thesis sentence at or near the end of your first paragraph. Your introductory paragraph will usually be rather short, approximately four or five sentences. It has a job to do, but once that's done, move on quickly to the body of your essay.

## Body Paragraphs

The paragraphs you have been practicing in this book are **body paragraphs**, the kind you use to provide the main part of your essays. As you know, they come in many modes and may be narrative, descriptive, and so on. Some essays may be entirely in one mode, but many will combine different modes in different paragraphs, using them as varied means to support a single thesis. Here is an example of a short essay using paragraphs of different kinds to support one overall thesis. Read the essay and then respond to the prompts that follow it.

## Student Essay: Do the Images of Women in Hip-Hop Harm Children?

MAVIS CAMPBELL

My aunt is an elementary teacher in a big city. She tells me all the time that the behavior of the children in her school gets worse every year. Second and third grade boys imitate hip-hop artists, calling girls "ho's," and little girls try to dress and dance like women they see on the latest DVDs. They think it is cool to imitate these degrading images of women. My aunt blames the culture of hip-hop. I agree with her: *It is time to protect children by insisting on a change in the way hip-hop artists treat women and talk about them.*

There's no way to deny it: At least some of the language and behavior that hip-hop artists direct at women is degrading. Of course some of the artists are super-talented and enormously popular. And they appeal to teenagers partly because they are in-your-face and refuse to conform to proper language and behavior. Who would listen to hip-hop if it didn't have anything "bad" in it? But when it shows women to be nothing but sex objects that men can insult and treat violently, it goes too far. It's one thing to be defiant toward authority figures like the police or the government, but attacking and insulting your own sisters and girlfriends isn't being cool.

When I mentioned this problem to a friend of mine who just came here from another country, he said, "This is America; it's a free country. Get used to it." And I've heard female hip-hop artists claim that it's up to the parents and the schools to influence the kids. If parents don't like what they hear and see, they insist, change the channel; don't let your kids see anything they shouldn't see. Artists say they just create what the public wants. The trouble with that argument is that these artists have a choice. They don't have to use such insulting language and treat women like prostitutes. They have just as much responsibility as parents and teachers. Years ago Reverend Calvin Butts in New York City hired a steam-roller to smash hundreds of rap albums because as a minister he recognized that popular music was forcing ministers, teachers, and parents to carry on a war against the influence of popular culture. He knew that individual parents and teachers can't do it alone. The problem has gotten much worse since Rev. Butts called attention to it. When the song "It's Hard Out Here for a Pimp," its insulting references to women, was performed at the Academy Awards, it sent a message to the whole country that demeaning women was acceptable. Then in 2007 when Don Imus made insulting remarks about the Rutgers women's basketball team, some people defended him by saying that he was just talking the way hip-hop performers do all the time. The lyrics of these songs have not improved since then and are likely to have a bad effect on the young.

In fact, hip-hop artists often have a stronger influence on small children than parents, teachers, or anyone else. Many kids don't have any responsible parents looking after them, and some parents work all the time. In addition, little kids imitate the older kids. So even if small children are not allowed to listen to hip-hop, they copy the way their friends and their older sisters and brothers talk and act. And these children know that successful hip-hop artists are rich, famous, and admired by almost everyone in their social group. How could they not end up copying the way they talk, dress, and behave? And faced with the hip-hop world of their older peer group members, these little girls see no choices in their future.

Therefore, artists shouldn't get away with saying they are not responsible for children's behavior. It's everybody's responsibility to care about children. Even hip-hop artists care about their own children. In his book called *From Pieces to Weight*, Fifty Cent says he didn't want his son to see his father being a street hustler and selling drugs because it would be a bad example for him. But some people would say that his attitude and the attitude of other hip-hop artists toward women set just as bad an example for their children. If people who manufacture and sell drugs have a bad influence on children, then people who create and sell CDs that treat women as prostitutes are also responsible for the harm they do to children.

I try to imagine my aunt going back to her school one day and seeing all the children working hard on their studies, dressing properly, showing respect for their teachers, and emulating inspiring role models. What would it take to make that happen? Of course, better supervision by parents and better schools would help, but my aunt is a great teacher, and that's not enough. It's hard to even imagine a school like that unless the culture of hip-hop changes enough to influence children in a better way.

1. State Mavis' thesis in your own words.
2. Explain the connection between the introductory paragraph and the concluding paragraph.
3. Identify three examples from real life that Mavis includes.
4. Identify a counterargument that she brings up and with which she disagrees.
5. Identify what you consider the strongest part of the essay.
6. Identify any weaknesses you see in the essay.
7. Explain why you agree or disagree with Mavis' opinion.

## Transitions Between Paragraphs

In the essay above, notice how Mavis uses the phrase *this problem* at the beginning of the third paragraph, the phrase *in fact* at the beginning of the fourth paragraph, and the word *therefore* at the beginning of the fifth paragraph. These devices, called **transitional words and phrases**, help link the paragraphs together.

To create continuity, use transitional words and phrases to guide the reader from one paragraph to the next. Where appropriate, connect the beginning of a body paragraph with the one before by using words like *however, therefore, next, another, by contrast, nevertheless, finally, more significantly, equally important, consequently,* and *similarly*. Think of these words as traffic signs that point helpful directions to drivers; without them, some drivers might find their way, but others will get lost.

## Concluding Paragraphs

Notice how Mavis ends her essay. Her **concluding paragraph** is rather short, but it does a lot, returning to the example of her aunt's school and reaffirming the main point of the essay. It also gives the reader a little extra food for thought by creating a picture in the imagination.

The closing paragraph of your essay will usually be shorter than the body paragraphs. It should reaffirm your thesis, perhaps referring to a phrase or thought from the first paragraph. But it should not use exactly the same words you have used before, and it should leave the reader with a sense of an ending. Reaching a strong conclusion does not mean that you should seem closed-minded, as if no one has a right to disagree with what you said. In fact, you should leave the reader with a lot to think about.

Neither is your ending the place to be changing your mind or altering your thesis. New ideas may occur to you while writing your concluding paragraph. If they cause you to rethink your thesis, you probably need another draft of your entire essay, with a rewritten thesis statement at the beginning and revised supporting paragraphs. Your final draft will then have a concluding paragraph that matches this new, improved thesis.

## Some Essay Topics

As you compose whole essays in advanced courses, remember all you have learned about paragraphs. Fully developed, clearly organized, well-written paragraphs are what it takes to build effective essays. Here is a list of essay topics that will give you the opportunity to create whole essays out of paragraphs.

### PERSONAL TOPICS (DESCRIPTIVE/NARRATIVE)

1. Tell about a person you misjudged. Explain how you came to understand that person's real character and how your relationship changed as a result.

2. Tell about a situation in which things were so bad that you almost gave up but, by persevering, overcame the difficulty. Explain what you learned from the experience.

3. Tell what it was like to take on some kind of responsibility that you were not prepared for, such as parenthood, a job, or a position of leadership. Explain what you learned about yourself in the process.

4. Describe three or four aspects of your family that you are proud of and several that you are not proud of. Explain how these characteristics determine your relationship to your family.

5. Create an essay portrait of a person you know who deserves to be better known for his or her personal qualities and actions. Explain how that person has influenced you.

6. Tell about a major change in your life, such as moving from one country to another, changing jobs, joining the military, or acquiring a new group of friends. Explain what you learned about yourself in the process.

7. Tell about several experiences with competition in your life and explain how they have affected your attitude toward competition and success.

## EXPLANATORY TOPICS

1. Tell about several changes that have occurred in one college or professional sport and explain how these changes have improved it or made it worse.
2. Describe two styles of dancing and explain what is similar and different about them. Describe the music used in each kind of dance, the way the partners relate to each other in the dance, and how easy or difficult it is to learn each style.
3. Describe and analyze the way young men and women relate to each other nowadays. Talk with an older relative and compare today's patterns of relating to the behavior of young men and women in a previous generation.
4. Explain what you like about cooking. Describe the kinds of food you like to prepare and explain what skills are needed to be an expert cook. Share with the reader the satisfactions that come from culinary expertise.
5. Explain how to play a game that you know well, such as chess or bridge. Include enough of your own experience to share with the reader the pleasures of playing the game well, the joy of winning, and the disappointment of losing.
6. Explain some of the factors that cause conflicts within families and some of the things family members can do to prevent and resolve them.
7. Explain some of the ways in which the use of social networks like Facebook has improved our lives and several ways it has made them worse. Use examples from your experience as part, but not all, of your supporting material.

## PERSUASIVE TOPICS

1. Argue whether or not young men and women should be required to do two years of national service, either in the military or in child care centers, senior centers, hospitals, schools, or homeless shelters. Include several methods of supporting your position, and explain why you are not convinced by the strongest argument on the opposing side.

2. Argue whether or not religious schools do a better job of educating children than public schools. Keep an open mind toward the arguments on the other side, and use several varied ways of supporting your position.

3. Argue whether it is better to live a high-risk life with the chance of wealth, excitement, and fame or a safer, more careful life with less risk but more modest and predictable gratifications.

4. Argue whether it is more important to be honest or to say what is advantageous to yourself in every situation. Explain whether honesty matters even in situations in which no one will know if you are lying.

5. Write an essay defending or opposing the existence of single-sex high schools. Explain why you think schools that enroll only girls or only boys will do a better or worse job of educating students.

6. Write an essay in which you agree or disagree with the statement, "It is no longer necessary to have a civil rights movement in the United States because racial equality has already been achieved."

7. Write an essay in which you agree or disagree with the this statement: "Big-time college sports bring many benefits—financial, social, and academic—to the universities that support them, and should be expanded."

## CREATIVE TOPICS

1. Imagine that you are the mayor of a large city. Explain some of the changes you would make in one area such as the school system, the transit system, business, and the justice system.

2. Write an imaginary conversation between you and a public figure with whose actions or opinions you disagree. Remember to use proper form for quotations.

3. Describe life in the United States fifty years from now. Concentrate on the kinds of changes that will probably take place in a few areas such as communications, transportation, entertainment, education, health care, economics, the environment, and the family.

4. If you could live at any time and place in the past, when and where would that be? Write an essay describing yourself living in that time and place. Explain how it would differ from your life now.

5. If you could make a film, what subject would you choose? Describe the film you would make—the story, the characters, and the setting. Explain why this particular film would appeal to you.

6. Write a letter to the author of a book you have enjoyed, telling him or her why the book meant so much to you and what you think he or she intended.

7. Pretend that you are one of your teachers or employers. Write a letter of recommendation explaining why a competitive college or professional school should admit you or why a particular company should hire you. Make your letter strong but honest,

# Writing Under Pressure: Facing Writing Examinations

Although you will be working on revision in the next chapter, there is one situation where you may not have enough time to do extensive revision—during a timed writing examination. Most of the work you have been doing assumes that you will write paragraphs and essays over a period of days during which you can develop drafts of your work, revise, and correct what you have written. You have been encouraged to read your work aloud to others and respond to their feedback.

All of this has to be put on hold, however, if you face, as most students in beginning courses do, a writing examination in which you have an hour, or at most two hours, to plan, create, and proofread an essay. If the examination essay is expected to be rather short and enough time is given for you to write a complete rough draft and revise it completely, you may find the whole process of revision useful. However, it is more common for students to plan, write, and correct one draft of an examination essay because the time is limited.

Exactly how you prepare for such a writing test depends very much on the specific test your institution requires. The most useful advice anyone can give you is for you to become as familiar as possible with all the requirements and expectations of the specific test you face. Ask your instructor about it, attend any special workshops offered that might prepare you for the test, and take practice exams if possible. Ask more advanced students who have passed the test for their advice, and find examples of model essays that provide a range from passing to exceptional.

Writing tests vary in type and approach. Some are given by the individual instructor, some are designed by a department, some are created and graded by the college or university, and some are created and supervised by testing companies. In some courses, your score on the test will be the only thing that determines whether you pass or fail. In other courses and institutions, your score will have a greater or lesser effect on your grade in the course. It will improve your chances greatly if you acquaint yourself with all the particulars of the test long before you take it. With all this in mind, you should remember certain points of advice about writing under pressure.

- Pressure is not all bad. A certain amount of pressure will force you to concentrate and probably perform better than you normally do—even though you may not feel better until you have completed your essay.
- Read the test directions carefully and be sure to follow them. Often failures happen because students simply do not pay enough attention to what they are asked to do on a writing test. If a question has several parts, be sure to complete both or all of them.
- Always do a little planning before writing, perhaps a rough outline of your main points. You may not have time to do elaborate pre-writing activities, but some brief planning always helps.
- Try to write steadily and carefully. Do not waste time, but don't rush either. You might be surprised at how many words you can write in only a half hour if you keep working. If you rush, however, you may start to panic and end up repeating yourself, writing many words but not saying much. Be sure to watch your paragraphs. Begin with a clear introductory paragraph that states your main purpose, and conclude with a final paragraph that sums up your idea. Be sure that the body of your essay is written in well-developed paragraphs that are unified, coherent, and written in varied, effective sentences.
- Always leave enough time to read over your work very carefully, especially if the test will be graded heavily on word and sentence correctness. It might even help to speak the words silently to yourself in order to catch any errors. Notice especially your first paragraph or two, where any errors will create an especially bad impression.

■ Visualize yourself succeeding and you probably will. What you have learned about writing will carry you through to higher levels. Each success leads to the next as your confidence in your writing skill grows.

## Key Words from Chapter 10 for Review

body paragraphs, concluding paragraph, introductory paragraph, thesis, thesis statement, topic sentences, transitional words and phrases

# Revising and Correcting Your Essays

---

## STEPPING UP: WRITING TIP 11

Beginning writers often think that revising and editing are the same thing. They know about correcting mistakes but are usually less familiar with the process of making larger changes to add material within paragraphs, rearranging subtopics, improving style, and even rethinking the main idea. Real **revision** calls for a whole new look at what you've written, and creating another whole draft of the essay, maybe two. In **editing**, on the other hand, is one of the last stages of the writing process: You have a draft of the essay that is as well argued and organized as you can make it, and all you want to do is to be sure there are no mistakes in word forms, spelling, phrasing, or sentence structure.

Revising comes first, then editing and proofreading. If you proofread too soon, you may not want to make necessary changes in your ideas, development, and organization.

---

# Revising for Unity and Coherence

Revising an essay is similar to revising paragraphs. That is, you should look carefully at your work, rethink your main idea and supporting material, and read your work aloud to others to see whether your writing is clear and effective. One difference, though, is that an essay requires even more attention to structure than a paragraph does, and once you have put together a whole essay, you will be even less eager to revise it than to revise a single paragraph. As with paragraphs, however, effective revision is the key to achieving your best writing.

One of the most common experiences in essay writing is for the writer to get to the final paragraph and discover a brilliant idea just as she or he is reaching a conclusion. If this happens to you, it may mean that, rather than tack this brilliant idea on to your last paragraph as an afterthought, you should rewrite the whole essay, using this new idea as your thesis statement in the first paragraph and developing through the rest of the essay. That's what real revision means: a complete makeover.

Why does this happen? Because writing is a way of thinking—one of the most effective ways, in fact. When we think in words, one idea leads us to another idea, and words suggest other words. As we write our way into a topic, we make discoveries. The biggest obstacle for many writers is their unwillingness to change what they have already written when new ideas occur to them. You may have to develop the habit of revising. It does not come naturally for everyone. Remember that the best writers tend to do the most revising, not because their early drafts are bad, but because they are such skilled writers that they can almost always see ways to improve their work.

Revising essays, like revising paragraphs, is not limited to correcting mistakes, even though editing and **correcting** are very important in the final stages of creating an essay. Still more important is the process of thinking and rethinking, developing, arranging, and rearranging material.

Two goals to strive for in making revisions are unity and coherence. **Unity** means staying on one main purpose, in other words, your thesis, throughout the essay and not wandering off the point. **Coherence** means making your essay hold together so that the reader always has a clear idea of where you're going; because that every part of the essay is where it belongs and there is an easy flow of ideas from one paragraph to the next. The best way to test whether your essay is unified and coherent is to read it aloud to another student or a small group and receive feedback on how easily they could follow your train of thought.

## PEER REVIEW QUESTIONS

Use these questions to help you and your classmates receive feedback from one another to help you revise the draft of your essays. Although one reader can help you revise, getting feedback from a number of classmates is usually more valuable.

### Peer Review Worksheet: Revising Essays for Unity and Coherence

1. You have a clear thesis and thesis statement.
   Yes _____ No _____

2. Your introduction and conclusion are clear and interesting. Yes _____ No _____

3. You stay on your thesis through the whole essay.
   Yes _____ No _____

4. You develop the topic very well _____ sufficiently _____ insufficiently _____.

5. I think your essay would benefit from the following kind(s) of revision:
   Rethinking your thesis: Yes _____
   No _____
   Including more supporting material: Yes _____
   No _____
   Improving your style and grammar: Yes _____
   No _____

6. What I liked best about your essay is the following:

7. I recommend that you make the following changes:

# Proofreading Practice: Applying What You've Learned

Most students understand the need for **proofreading**, but it is easy to become impatient and not take the time to read through our work carefully for mistakes. In an age when most people on a moment's notice fire off e-mail messages with incorrect spelling, grammar, and punctuation, we can easily forget to proofread our formal writing carefully.

It helps to use correct language at all stages of the writing process. Meticulous proofreading, however, comes at the final stage. In earlier stages, before making revisions for unity and coherence, it's not helpful to worry too much about surface errors because doing so will interfere with making larger decisions about content and organization. But there is definitely a time for careful proofreading—after you have made your larger revisions in organization and content.

Proofreading is usually most effective if you do it slowly as you read your work aloud. To be a good proofreader, you will need to know how accurate your grasp of grammar, punctuation, and spelling is. The exercises that follow will give you an opportunity to test and review your mastery of correct grammar and usage by spotting errors of different kinds within passages of writing on various topics. Try to identify the errors that occur most often in your own writing and keep working on finding and correcting them.

## Paragraph with Proofreading Corrections

Read the paragraph below and note the kinds of corrections the writer made while proofreading.

*struck*
The 9.0 magnitude earthquake that strike near the northeast coast of
*forced*
Japan on March 11, 2011 was so severe that it has force experts to
*their*
change there thinking about coping with natural disasters. The quake
*Japan. The shock*
was the worst in more than a century for Japan, the shock was so
*were*
severe that the nearby city of Sendai was devastated, as where many

towns and villages in the region. Even in Tokyo, 200 miles away, build-
*trembled*
ings tremble. The tsunami that followed destroyed countless homes

across the coast, leaving thousands of people without shelter. Power
*occurred*
outages occur in many towns and villages, and the Fukushima Daiichi
*seriously*
nuclear plant was damaged so serious that radioactive leakage oc-

curred. Then a month later, another 7.1 earthquake struck, causing
*closed*
two more nuclear plants to be close. As a result of the two quakes,
*missing, and the*
tens of thousands of people were killed or listed as missing, the
*take a long*
extent of harm caused by damage to the nuclear plants may take long

time to determine. As a result of this disaster, not only the Japanese

*taking*

government but governments and experts around the world are taken

*putting*

another look at the safety of nuclear plants and puting strategies in

place for coping with future earthquakes and other natural disasters.

## TEST YOURSELF: Editing for Sentence Errors in Context

Examine the boldfaced italic spots in the passage below. If the sentence division is correct, leave it as it is. If not, correct the punctuation to eliminate fragments, comma splices, or run-on sentences.

Cameron's schedule keeps him busy all week *long, he* is on the go from morning until night. On Mondays and Wednesdays he has to arrive at his job at 8:00 *a.m., this* means that he must get up at 6:30. He drives five miles to the computer store where he works, *and* he usually takes fifteen minutes looking for a parking place. He works until 4:00 in the *afternoon after* that he drives three miles to the campus. On these evenings he has dinner in the student union and goes to class from 6:00 to 9:00. On Tuesdays, Thursdays, and Fridays his schedule is even *busier, on* those days he gets up at 5:30 and begins an early shift at 7:00. Then at 3:00 p.m. he hurries from his job to a business class that begins at 4:00, which is followed by his history *class this* means he doesn't have dinner until 6 o'clock. On Tuesdays and Thursdays he usually does homework in the late *evening, but* on Friday nights he is always with his girlfriend Karen.

*Answers:* 1. long. He 2. 8:00 a.m.; this means **or** 8:00 a.m. This means 3. , and he (correct) 4. afternoon; after that **or** afternoon. After that 5. busier; on these days **or** busier. On these days 6. history class; this means **or** history class. This means 7. evening, but (correct)

## WRITING EXERCISES: Basic, Intermediate, Challenge

# Basic Exercise: Editing for Sentence Errors in Context

Examine the boldfaced italic spots in the passage below. If the sentence division is correct, leave it as it is. If not, correct the punctuation to eliminate fragments, comma splices, or run-on sentences.

Amanda has more pets than anyone I **know, she** also has some of the most unusual pets. Her favorite pet, for instance, is her ocelot named **Sphinx this** is a kind of wild cat that most people wouldn't want in their homes. She also has a ferret, which slithers and slinks around her **apartment. Half** of the time she can't find it until it comes out from under the sofa to eat. Then there is her baby snake that she named **Satan, it** is a boa constrictor that is still small but will get very large someday. Her parrot, named Pavarotti, can't sing in spite of his **name, but** he talks all day long. She also has some ordinary **pets. Including** a chubby poodle and a hamster. The most boring of her animals is her **goldfish, however**, it is the easiest one to take care of.

## Intermediate Exercise: Editing for Sentence Errors in Context

Examine the passage that follows. Correct the punctuation to eliminate fragments, comma splices, and run-on sentences. If a punctuation mark is correct, let it stand.

Online courses have drawbacks as well as advantages. Distance learning is not a miracle as some people once expected it is not a disaster as others predicted. Some colleges hoped to save large amounts of money by offering courses on the Web, however the costs are not as low as anticipated. Many students thought that taking courses electronically would be easy. That they would do less work than in other classes. Both expectations turned out to be wrong, online courses are not easier than classroom courses, and they do not require less work. On the other hand, some students benefit greatly from online instruction. Students with difficult schedules can always fit an online course into their program, in addition, those who are shy about speaking up in class often participate actively in online discussion boards. Institutions also take advantage of online instruction for example, they can offer courses to nonmatriculated students from all over the country and save on classroom space. Courses taught online seem unlikely to drive out classroom instruction, nevertheless they will probably remain a permanent feature of higher education.

# Challenge Exercise: Editing for Sentence Errors in Context

Examine the passage that follows. Correct the punctuation to eliminate fragments, comma splices, and run-on sentences. If a punctuation mark is correct, let it stand.

*Affirmative action* is a term used to describe efforts to increase ethnic diversity in college admissions and employment. Since the 1960s there has been controversy over the consideration of race in admissions, not surprisingly, there have been opponents and defenders of affirmative action. Defenders usually point out that special efforts are needed to increase the number of minority students at many institutions. While opponents insist that we should have a color-blind society and not look at race in admission or hiring. One case that has remained important in this debate is the Bakke case in 1978, in this case the Supreme Court decided that a medical school could take race into consideration but not by means of a quota system. More recently, the Supreme Court in June 2003 issued two rulings, one of them supported the University of Michigan's Law School admissions policy of considering race along with other factors. The other struck down the undergraduate admissions procedures at Michigan in this case the policy was to use a point system for ranking candidates. In 2007 the Supreme Court also ruled that public schools could not assign students by race in the effort to integrate schools. Despite such reversals in the United States, the principle of affirmative action has been adopted by many countries in Europe, Asia, and South America, it has also been supported by the United Nations Committee on Human Rights. The ultimate question is how much racial injustice still exists in most countries, people will continue to give different answers to that question.

---

## TEST YOURSELF: Editing for Phrasing Errors in Context

Find and correct the seven errors in the following passage. Look for mistakes in agreement, parallel structure, or **phrasing**. Do the whole exercise before looking at the answers.

Victor has a risk-taking personality. Since he was a child, he has always been involved in activities that is either physically dangerous or likely to be costly in other ways. When he was still in elementary school, he would dive off high rocks into a lake near his home, and when he was only eight years old, he once hopped on a motorcycle and rode it a half-mile. As an adolescent, he won skateboard competitions until he dislocated one day his shoulder. He has always gambled—on cards, sporting events, video games, horses, and he bought lottery tickets. As a young man he worked at a race track to earn enough money to visit Las Vegas, in which he learned to work in a casino as a croupier. He began to gamble and lost so much money that he had to leave Las Vegas and return home. Since then he has lost money many times, fallen from a hang glider, smashed up three race cars, and a broken leg while ski jumping. In the future he wants to take on the challenge of creating a business. He plans to earn a degree in business administration which he hopes to start a Web consulting company that will help people invest in high-technology stocks. He believes that a risk-taking person may sometimes fail but they will always come back. So far, he has managed to do that.

*Answers:* 1. activities that are 2. one day he dislocated 3. horses, and lottery tickets 4. Las Vegas, where he 5. and broken a leg while ski jumping 6. after which he hopes to start 7. but he or she will always come back

WRITING EXERCISES: Basic, Intermediate, Challenge

## Basic Exercise: Editing for Phrasing Errors in Context

There are seven phrasing errors in bold print in the following passage. Explain how these mistakes in agreement, parallel structure, or phrasing should be corrected.

Some people like to talk about their pet peeves. Alexia **prefer** to talk about her "faves" instead. These are her favorite things that happen or that people **does** which make her feel better about herself and other people. She isn't referring to big things like getting rich or **she just met** her lifetime soulmate. Her faves are the small things **which they** make her life happier, for example, little compliments, like somebody telling her they like the colors of her scarf or the way she just changed her hairdo. She also likes unexpected bits of good luck, such as finding a pair of gloves she thought she lost, discovering that her term paper is due a week later than she expected, or **to have** a bus arrive just as she reaches the bus stop. She also is especially fond of surprises like surprise parties, unexpected gifts that people give her for no particular reason, and unanticipated e-mail messages from people she **haven't** heard from in a long time. She always wonders **how could she** keep her spirits up if she didn't have these little things to make her feel better.

## Intermediate Exercise: Editing for Phrasing Errors in Context

Find and correct the seven errors in the following passage. Look for mistakes in agreement, parallel structure, or phrasing.

Psychologists try to use scientific methods to prove their theories. Unlike physicists or chemists, however, psychologists requires human subjects for most of their experiments, but human beings cannot be analyzed in a laboratory like chemicals or electrical equipment. In the past, considerably more latitude was permitted in conducting experiments on people. In recent years, however, strict criteria has been established to limit the possibilities for testing that use human subjects. As a result, many of the experiments that they became famous in the twentieth century, such as Stanley Milgram's experiments testing whether people would obey orders to inflict electrical shocks on others, would be prohibited today. Equally less likely to be allowed would be the cruel experiments on animals that was conducted in the past, especially those on monkeys and chimpanzees. Such restrictions may seem to retard, complicate, and discouraging the pursuit of psychological knowledge. Nevertheless, the consensus is that the attempt to understand the human mind and alleviate mental illness does not justify we inflict harm on human beings or animals.

## Challenge Exercise: Editing for Phrasing Errors in Context

Find and correct the seven errors in the following passage. Look for mistakes in agreement, parallel structure, or phrasing.

Filmmaking have changed a lot over the last century. The first silent films look crude and awkward to us today, but they provided exciting entertainment in its time. In the early 1900s

D. W. Griffith developed techniques like close-up shots, shots from many angles, and he used cross-cutting, which means moving quickly from one scene to another. Such techniques and others were developed in silent films made not just in Hollywood but also in France, Germany, Russia, and the Scandinavian countries. With the invention of sound, which were first used in *The Jazz Singer* (1927), motion pictures took on another dimension. Films of the 1930s included musicals, gangster films, horror films, and they made wonderful comedies. World War II brought the creation of propaganda films, newsreels, and a whole series of realistic films of the postwar period. In the 1950s, brief experiments was tried with wide screens and three-dimensional effects which required viewers to wear special glasses. At the same time, art films from abroad became popular, especially among intellectuals. Science fiction films, of which many had been made since the early years, became enormously popular in the sixties and seventies. Since then, Hollywood films have attracted the largest audiences through spectacular special effects, enhanced since the 1990s through computer graphics as in *Jurassic Park* (1993). The development from *The Great Train Robbery* in 1903 to *The Lord of the Rings* in 2003 and the return of 3D effects in *Avatar* in 2009 have been extraordinary in both technology and artistry

---

## TEST YOURSELF: Editing for Word Errors in Context

Find and correct the seven errors in the following passage. Look for mistakes in word forms, spelling, capitalization, apostrophes, and word choice. Do the whole exercise before looking at the answers.

Our college should build a residence hall for students who can't commute to class from their homes. This would benefit all of the student in several ways. Students from other States and other countries might attend the college, and they would make our classes and extracurricular activities more interesting. Young students still living at home with their parents sometimes can't study because their are younger brothers and sister making noise, watching television, and using the computer. If they lived in a dormitory, they could study more and set example for other students, thereby raising the academic standards of the college. Some students from wealthier families might be attracted to the school because of the dormitory. They wouldn't need no scholarship aid, and their families might contribute money to the college. Most of all, a dormitory would make the college a more social place that would seem like a home for all students. This would give the whole college a more stronger feeling of identity and make the graduates feel so loyal that they would contribute money later.

*Answers:* 1. all of the student**s** 2. from other **s**tates 3. because ***there*** are 4. brothers and sister**s** 5. set ***an*** example 6. wouldn't need ***any*** scholarship aid 7. a ***stronger*** feeling of identity

WRITING EXERCISES: Basic, Intermediate, Challenge

## Basic Exercise: Editing for Word Errors in Context

Find and correct the seven errors in the following passage. Look for mistakes in word forms, spelling, capitalization, apostrophes, and word choice.

Samantha thinks that her dream of becoming a physical therapist is the right goal for her. She work as a volunteer in a senior residence, where she often has to help people cope with there physical limitations. She was once in a bicycle accident, in which she broke her leg and had to stay off her feet for three weeks. A physical Therapist visited her and taught her exercises to practice walking again. Samantha was so impress with how much the therapist knew and how efficiently she taught her the exercises that she started asking questions about physical therapy as career. The therapist told her about some Web sites, where she found out more about what physical therapists do and what kind of educational background and training they need. Because she has always been athletic and interested in coaching and helping people improve their skills, she can't think of a more better career for herself then becoming a physical therapist.

## Intermediate Exercise: Editing for Word Errors in Context

Find and correct the seven errors in the following passage. Look for mistakes in word forms, spelling, capitalization, apostrophes, and word choice.

Homeschooling has become popular everywhere from Arizona to maine, but it is to early to know whether it is mostly a success or a failure. Many parent in the past few years have decided to homeschool their children. Some of them do it for religious reasons, and others think the public schools are not safe. Some also think they can educate there children better than the schools can. Some of these students have been in the news when they excelled in spelling contest or achieved other honors, such as being admitted to the most competetive colleges. On the other hand, there have been cases of child abuse linked to homeschooling. It is time for experts to do serious research so they can find out whether homeschooling should be encourage, changed, or stopped.

## Challenge Exercise: Editing for Word Errors in Context

Find and correct the seven errors in the following passage. Look for mistakes in word forms, spelling, capitalization, apostrophes, and word choice.

Students who wish to major in business Administration take courses in two categories of economics—macroeconomics and microeconomics. Sometimes these two aspects are included in the same course; sometimes they are taught in seperate courses. Macroeconomics include such large elements of economics as changes in the gross national product, interest rates, globalization, and inflation. Microeconomics pays more closer attention to how prices are determined, how consumers make choices, how worker select jobs, and how other patterns occur within a particular economic system. Both areas of study have to do with business, supply and demand, and production of goods and services, but they focusing on different scales of economic activity. Professors approaches may differ, but there is always a distinction between these two general areas of economics.

## Key Words from Chapter 11 for Review

coherence, correcting, editing, phrasing, proofreading, revision, unity

# Some Fine Points

---

### STEPPING UP: WRITING TIP 12

Many writers in our age of text-processing and computer spelling checks pay less attention to their own spelling skills than they should. Although electronic spelling checks are extremely useful, they will not always prevent you from making embarrassing errors. Remember that if you misspell a word by confusing one word with another, your spelling check will not catch the error. And what about handwritten letters and college tests? There is still a need to become proficient in spotting errors. It is especially important to master the words that look alike because they are mostly very common words that your computer may not catch when you misuse them. The good news is that you know most of these look-alikes already; just study the ones you do not already know.

---

## Spelling

The key to correct spelling is to know yourself. Are you a strong speller who can confidently trust yourself to judge words by the way they look to you? Or are you a weak speller who needs to continually look up words you may have misspelled? Some excellent writers are weak spellers who need to rely constantly on their spell check and dictionary. Although bad spelling may not make you a bad writer in other respects, your professors may make initial judgments about your written work based on your spelling. Correct spelling in a document creates a favorable first impression of that document; on the other hand, incorrect spelling—especially of words commonly used in college-level writing or of words whose spellings can be confused—causes the reader to lose faith in the writer. Why should your intended audience take seriously what you have to say in a persuasive essay when the third word of your first sentence is misspelled?

The most important thing you can do to improve your spelling is to make a list of the common words you misspell and work on them until you know them. These words will differ somewhat with each writer, but certain words tend to cause trouble for many people. Go over the list that follows and be sure to master any spellings you do not know.

## Commonly Misspelled Words

| | | |
|---|---|---|
| achieve | develop | recommend |
| across | familiar | responsibility |
| address | fulfill | separate |
| athlete | immediately | similar |
| beginning | jewelry | society |
| believe | necessary | suppose |
| committed | occasionally | until |
| decision | occurrence | |
| definitely | receive | |

---

## TEST YOURSELF: Spelling

Find and correct the misspelled word in each sentence.

1. I intend to work until I acheive all of my goals.
2. The beginning of the game was definitly exciting.
3. Every student will fulfill his or her responsability.
4. People who develope their talents benefit society.
5. It is occasionally necessary to make a quick deceison.
6. The sisters were familar with the separate aspects of the project.
7. The store sent the jewlery to the wrong address.

*Answers:* 1. achieve 2. definitely 3. responsibility 4. develop 5. decision 6. familiar
7. jewelry

## Basic Exercise: Spelling

Find and correct the one misspelled word in each sentence. Consult the list of commonly misspelled words when you are not sure of a particular spelling.

1. Robert and Sam have similiar beliefs about success.
2. Susan is definitely commited to this project.
3. That address is directly accross from the bank.
4. Keep going untill you reach a familiar spot.
5. They took seperate roads but both achieved success.
6. She occassionally makes important decisions on her own.
7. The best atheletes receive scholarships from the college.

## Intermediate Exercise: Spelling

In each of the following sentences, there may or may not be one mis-spelled word. Find and correct all misspelled words. Consult the list of commonly misspelled words when you are not sure of a particular spelling.

1. Kenneth is familar with most important films made since the beginning of the film industry.
2. He studied what the silent filmmakers were able to achieve from 1900 untill the advent of sound in the late 1920s.
3. By concentrating on conveying messages entirely through visual images, he thought, the silent filmmakers were able to develope a high level of expression.
4. Kenneth discovered that silent films were made in many coun-tries accross the world, including France, Argentina, Japan, India, and Australia.
5. He definitely likes the classic films of the 1930s and 1940s, when Hollywood became a magical place and a source of myths for American society.
6. He also recomends foreign films of the 1950s and 1960s to his friends.
7. He thinks it is wrong to suppose that the cinema has already full-filed its potential; he is sure it will develop more techniques in the future.

## Challenge Exercise: Spelling

In each of the following sentences, there may be up to two misspelled words; however, in some sentences there may be only one or none at all. Find and correct all misspelled words *without consulting the list.*

1. Although this is the space age, most people are not familar with the cosmos.
2. Most people, for example, know only a little about the begining of the universe and similiar astronomical phenomena.
3. To acheive such knowledge, it is not neccesary to take an entire course in astronomy.
4. Many popular books and scientific magazines are definitly sufficient to keep any ordinary person informed about the latest discoveries.
5. Science fiction has led many of us to surpose that it will be easy to launch manned spaceships beyond the solar system immediately.
6. However, to travel accross the huge distances involved, it would be necessary to develope new forms of propulsion.
7. What seems easy in fiction is definately not so easy in real life, but we are committed to learning as much as we can about the cosmos; it is our responsability.

# Capitalization

Knowing when to use capital and lowercase letters is very simple—and very complicated. The simple rule is that **common nouns** begin with lowercase letters and **proper nouns** (see Parts of Speech, p. 137) begin with uppercase, or capital, letters. That is, you should capitalize names of *specific* persons, institutions, places, countries, cities, and so on. For example, capitalize *France* (*specific* country), *Intel* (*specific* company), *President Obama* (*specific* person), *New York City* (*specific* city), etc. But use lowercase for words like *nation, company, woman, metropolis,* and the like.

Sounds easy, doesn't it? Then why is complicated? Sometimes it's hard to decide whether a word is general or specific. One common example is the difference between the names of months, which are all capitalized (*January, February, March*), as are the days of the week (*Monday, Tuesday, Wednesday*), and the names of the seasons, which are not: *spring, summer, fall, winter.* Another common distinction is between the titles of specific college courses, which are capitalized

(*Economics 101, Philosophy 300, Literature of Diversity*), and general references to subjects (a course in *economics*, a major in *philosophy*, an exam in *business*). When you are not sure whether to capitalize a noun, look it up in the dictionary. If it's a specific name that cannot be found in the dictionary, you should capitalize it.

Another tricky problem is knowing how to capitalize words in titles of books, articles, and movies. Always capitalize the first and last word in a title, and all other words except the very short prepositions, articles, and connective words (see Parts of Speech, p. 137), such as *and, the, a, an, in, of,* and *with*. For example, capitalize as follows: *Gone with the Wind, A Raisin in the Sun, Sex and the City.*

---

### TEST YOURSELF: Capitalization

Identify a word in each sentence that should be capitalized.

1. I am majoring in economics, but first I have to take mathematics 150.
2. When my sister visited ghana, she took along her cousin.
3. Henry may not finish his master's thesis by march, but he certainly will by summer.
4. As a high school student, Rosa worked at mcdonald's during the summer.
5. One event during the civil rights movement was the montgomery bus boycott.
6. The whole class read a classical play called *antigone.*
7. The astronomy course paid special attention to the planet mars.

*Answers:* 1. Mathematics 150 2. Ghana 3. March 4. McDonald's 5. Montgomery
6. *Antigone* 7. Mars

---

### WRITING EXERCISES: Basic, Intermediate, Challenge

## Basic Exercise: Capitalization

Identify one word in each sentence that should be capitalized. One sentence is correct.

1. Sheila liked her astronomy course, but she was less pleased with psychology 100.
2. Before moving to denver, Sally had lived in three western states.
3. The spring carnival will take place in april, but last year it was delayed.
4. Please stop at johnson's bakery on your way home from the university.

5. Robert read *Andersonville* for his history class.
6. The lecture on civil rights will take place on tuesday.
7. Most of the patients were treated by dr. Carson.

## Intermediate Exercise: Capitalization

Identify one word in each sentence that should either be changed to a capital letter or be reduced to lowercase. One sentence is correct.

1. The weather was so warm in September that we expected a mild Autumn.
2. Sylvia decided to sell her toyota and lease a Mitsubishi.
3. The class will be discussing *Death Of a Salesman.*
4. Walking toward the student union, Stanley saw his economics professor.
5. Many government officials in washington maintain two residences.
6. In her handbag Diane found a ten dollar bill, her cell phone, and a ticket to the knicks game.
7. During his meeting with the dean of the College, Thomas explained why he had organized the protest.

## Challenge Exercise: Capitalization

Identify one or two words in each sentence that should either be changed to a capital letter or be reduced to lowercase. One sentence is correct.

1. Students who major in Business should take mathematics 210.
2. The title *The great Gatsby* was not the one that F. Scott Fitzgerald first chose for his Novel.
3. The Department of sociology at Kansas State university is large.
4. Reading books and articles on Psychology increases one's Awareness.
5. Not only the United States but also European countries and Japan have explored Mars.
6. Psychologists once referred to bipolar disorder as Manic-depression.
7. The problems of Northern Ireland stem from conflicts between catholics and protestants.

# Look-Alikes

Some common words that we use every day get mixed up with each other because they look or sound alike. One of the most frequent mix-ups is in confusing the words *there* and *their*. Following is a short list of the **look-alikes** that are most often mixed up. Study them, take the Test Yourself quiz, and practice writing sentences using all of them correctly. More importantly, notice how you use them in your own writing assignments and be alert to those that you habitually get mixed up.

Please remember, too, that when you write on a computer, the spell check will not catch most of these mix-ups. If you use *were* instead of *where*, or *principle* instead of *principal*, the spell check may not pick up the mistake because the word you wrote is a correctly spelled word when used in a different way.

## Basic Look-Alikes

The words on this list are easy to tell apart and easy to use, but they cause many mistakes when writers are careless. Study them to be sure you know which is which, and, even more important, watch to see that you use them correctly in your writing.

| | |
|---|---|
| 1. **a lot, allot** | Always write *a lot* as two words: We need *a lot* of financial backing. There is no such word as *alot*. The word *allot,* with two *l*'s, means "to distribute": Please *allot* the same amount to each member of the committee. |
| 2. **a, an, and** | Use *a* before consonants, *an* before vowels: *a* computer, but *an* old computer. Use *an* before words beginning with silent *h*: *an* honest worker. Use *a* before *u* words that start with a *y* sound: *a* union leader. Use *a* before *one* because of the *w* sound: *a* one-cylinder motor. The rule is to use *a* before consonant *sounds* and *an* before vowel *sounds*. *And* is the connective word: Sam *and* his wife. |
| 3. **bought, brought** | Be sure to write these as they sound: *bought* is the past tense of *buy*: We *bought* a surfboard. *Brought* is the past tense of *bring*: I *brought* it to the beach. |
| 4. **buy, by** | To *buy* is to purchase: We *buy* merchandise. *By* is a preposition: We often pass *by* the museum. |
| 5. **does, dose** | Notice the spelling and the sound: *does* sounds like *duzz*: She *does* everything. *Dose* rhymes with *close*: a *dose* of medicine. Notice the spelling of *doesn't* (not *dosen't*). |

| 6. **have, of** | Don't write "I would *of* enjoyed that." It should be "I would *have* enjoyed that." Watch all those *should have, might have, must have, could have* combinations. *Have* sounds like *of* in some phrases: she *should've* been here—short for *should have.* |
|---|---|
| 7. **fine, find, fined** | *Fine* means "excellent": She was a *fine* dancer. To *find* means to locate: *Find* a date for your cousin. *Fined* (pronounced the same as *find*) means to be ordered to pay a *fine*: She was *fined* for double parking. |
| 8. **its, it's** | *Its* shows possession; *it's* is short for *it is* or *it has*: The jury made *its* decision. *It's* a cool day for July. *It's* (it has) been an entertaining evening. There is no such word as *its'*. |
| 9. **than, then** | Use *than* for comparisons: funnier *than* Eddie Murphy. Use *then* for time: *Then* we started dancing. |
| 10. **to, too, two** | *Two*, the number, is usually spelled right: There were *two* cars in the garage. The trick is to know when to use *too*. Remember that *too*, with *more* than one *o*, means *more* than enough: There is *too* much noise here. It also means in addition: You come *too*. All the other meanings take *to*: travel *to* Cuba; *to* win at poker. |

---

## TEST YOURSELF: Basic Look-Alikes

Write the correct word in each blank.

1. (to, too, two)    Sonya thought it was _____ hot
_____ take her _____ dogs
to the park.

2. (a, an, and)    The honk of _____ automobile horn
startled _____ flock of pigeons
_____ made them fly away.

3. (its, it's)    I can tell that _____ going to rain when
my parrot rattles _____ cage.

4. (have, of)    You could _____ demanded a more
interesting kind _____ job.

| 5. (than, then) | Mike was taller _____ his brother _____, but now they are the same height. |
| 6. (buy, by) | Andrea had to pass _____ her old boyfriend's house in order to _____ groceries. |
| 7. (find, fine, fined) | Hector had a _____ time at the party but couldn't _____ his car keys and was afraid he'd be _____ for double parking. |

*Answers:* 1. too, to, two 2. an, a, and 3. it's, its 4. have, of 5. than, then 6. by, buy 7. fine, find, fined

## Intermediate Look-Alikes

The words on this list are a bit more challenging, but equally likely to cause frequent errors. One pair, *their* and *there*, in fact, causes the most frequent mix-ups of all.

| 1. **advice, advise** | Pronounce them correctly and you will spell them correctly: *Advice* contains the word *ice*: You give *advice* (a noun). *Advise* rhymes with *wise* and is a verb: You *advise* someone. |
| 2. **affect, effect** | *Affect* is the verb: This *affects* all of us. *Effect* is the noun: What is the *effect* of crime? (Exception: *effect* can sometimes be a verb meaning "to bring about or create": Let's *effect* an improvement in communications.) |
| 3. **always, away** | These do not sound alike, but because they look similar, many writers mistakenly write *alway*. Don't drop the *s*. |
| 4. **choose, chose** | The present form is *choose*—rhymes with *news*: I *choose* a different program each week. *Chose* is the past tense—rhymes with *rose*: Last month we *chose* the spot for our vacation. |
| 5. **know, no, now** | *Know* and *no* sound alike and are often confused. *Now* (rhymes with *cow*) and means "at present": We are *now* in the fourth act. Remember the word *knowledge*—that which you *know*. Don't write, I *no* how to swim. |

6. **mind, mine, mines**  Don't confuse *mine* (belonging to me) with *mind* (a smart *mind*). Although *mines* is widely spoken in dialect, there is no such pronoun in standard written English. (That pen is *mine*, not *mines*.) *Mines* are holes in the ground, like gold *mines*.

7. **our, are, or**  *Our* is possessive—belonging to us: *our* schedules. Don't confuse it with the verb *are*: Sally and Timothy *are* married. *Or* is a connective word: Either Tom *or* Randy will wait for you.

8. **quiet, quit, quite**  Notice the extra syllable in *quiet*, meaning "silent": The room was *quiet*. (*Quiet* rhymes with *diet*.) To *quit* (rhymes with *hit*) means to stop: He *quit* his job. *Quite* (rhymes with *white*) means *very*: She is *quite* talented.

9. **they, their, they're, there**  The word *they* is used as a subject, referring to a number of people or things: *They* belong to the gang. *Their* means belonging to them: *Their* ideas are right. *They're* is short for *they are*: *They're* going to be rich. *There* means at that place, or it may be just a structure word: *There* is a new hairstyle this year.

10. **you're, your**  *You're* is short for *you are*: *You're* never home when I call. *Your* shows possession: *Your* contract is in the mail.

---

## TEST YOURSELF: Intermediate Look-Alikes

Write the correct word in each blank.

1. (know, no, now)    In the past, business schools did not require students to _____ much higher mathematics, but _____ a student with _____ mathematics courses would be at a great disadvantage.

2. (affect, effect)

Theresa underestimated the
_____ of her college degree.
She thought it would _____
only her salary.

3. (their, there, they're)

The children enjoy _____
after-school activities. This week
_____ learning how to paint,
and _____ are two other
projects planned.

4. (advice, advise)

When the financial _____
Ted gave his brother turned out to
be correct, he decided that he would
_____ other people about
their investments.

5. (quiet, quit, quite)

Sandra was planning to _____
her job, but she kept _____
about it for _____ a while.

6. (your, you're)

If _____ planning to major in
accounting, speak to _____
adviser about it.

7. (mind, mine, mines)

Delores wouldn't _____
doing your taxes; she always does
_____.

*Answers:* 1. know, now, no 2. effect, affect 3. their, they're, there 4. advice, advise
5. quit, quiet, quite 6. you're, your 7. mind, mine

## Challenge Look-Alikes

The words on this list are still more difficult to tell apart and spell correctly. However, they are also words that you will use frequently, so be sure to master any of them that you do not know how to spell.

1. **conscience, conscious**

Your *conscience* (pronounce it: kon shuntz) is your sense of right and wrong: Let your *conscience* be your guide. To be *conscious* (kon shuss) is to be aware: She was *conscious* of someone approaching.

2. **convenience, convince**

Listen to the sound: *convenience* (kunveen-yuntz). I'll do it at your *convenience*. I'll *convince* (kun *vintz*) you to buy it.

3. **lead, led**

*Lead* (or *leads*)—rhymes with *need*—is present tense: I usually *lead* the trumpet section. *Led* is the past tense: She *led* (rhymes with *red*) the parade last year. However, the metal *lead*, as in a *lead* pipe, is pronounced the same as *led*.

4. **loose, lose, loss, lost**

Pronunciation is the key again. *Loose*, meaning "not tight," rhymes with *moose*: The nails had come *loose*. *Lose* is the verb, rhyming with *fuse*: Don't *lose* your temper. *Loss* is a noun: One *loss* won't affect your league standings. (*Loss* rhymes with *boss*.) *Lost* (rhymes with *cost*) means "gone": They were *lost* in the forest.

5. **pass, passed, past**

The verb is *pass* (present tense) and *passed* (past tense): I *pass* the store every day; I *passed* all my courses last semester. Use *past* as the noun or the preposition: She lives in the *past*. We drove *past* her house.

6. **principal, principle**

Remember that *principle* (it has *le* like *rule*) refers to a rule or law: the *principle* of gravity. *Principal* means "important": the *principal* of the school, the *principal* part in a play.

7. **taught, thought**

Master this difficult pair by pronouncing each word carefully. *Taught* (rhymes with *fought*) is the past tense of *teach*: She *taught* calculus. *Thought* (rhymes with *bought*) is the past tense of *think*: We *thought* it was a good restaurant.

8. **threw, through**

*Threw* (rhymes with *new*) is the past tense of *throw*: We *threw* a big party. Don't mix up *threw* and *through*; they sound the same. *Through* means finished (when they were *through* eating) or inside (*through* the tunnel).

9. **we're, were, where**    *We're* is short for *we are: We're* the first people here. *Were* is a verb: *Were* those books expensive? *Where* asks about the place something happens: *Where* did you go last night? Don't mix up *where* and *were*. They look similar but don't sound alike.

10. **worse, worst**    Both are forms of *bad: bad, worse, worst.* Use *worse* to compare two things, persons, or situations: Her illness became *worse*. This film is *worse* than the other one. *Worst* is the superlative form; it describes one thing that stands out from the rest: the *worst* dinner I ever ate; the *worst* car in the lot.

## TEST YOURSELF: Challenge Look-Alikes

Write the correct word in each blank.

1. (principal, principle)    Clearly, the _____ reason why James left his job was not money; he acted on _____.

2. (convenience, convince)    It was easy to _____ Karen to see the _____ of using a debit card.

3. (pass, passed, past)    Remembering his _____ performance, Jason thought he could _____ the math test. He had already _____ the writing test.

4. (taught, thought)    The film _____ lessons about history, but some critics _____ it was somewhat slow-moving.

5. (conscience, conscious)    Although he was _____ of Paul's motives, Trevor's _____ would not let him reveal the secret.

6. (worse, worst)    As the storm got _____ and _____, the weather control advised people to prepare for the _____.

7. (we're, were,
    where)

Do you know _____ we
_____ when you lost the scarf?
Unless you remember, _____ not
going to find it.

*Answers:* 1. principal, principle 2. convince, convenience 3. past, pass, passed
4. taught, thought 5. conscious, conscience 6. worse, worse, worst 7. where, were,
we're

WRITING EXERCISES: Basic, Intermediate, Challenge

## Basic Exercise: Look-Alikes

Circle the word in parentheses that correctly completes each sentence.

1. The story contains (a lot, allot) of humor, but it has (a, an) unhappy ending.
2. She should (have, of) placed the books (were, where) we could easily (find, fine) them.
3. If you want to (buy, by) good audio equipment, (it's, its) a good idea to shop around.
4. The crowd was (to, too, two) loud, but, rather (than, then) leave, we moved (to, too, two) (a, an) different table.
5. Stanley (bought, brought) a CD at the store, then tried to (find, fine) his way home.
6. This math test (doesn't, dosen't) appear (to, too, two) difficult for Hector.
7. She should (have, of) told me that she is younger (than, then) her brother.

## Intermediate Exercise: Look-Alikes

Circle the word in parentheses that correctly completes each sentence.

1. The political leaders in (are, our) city (always, away) (know, no) how to exploit the media.
2. The (advice, advise) of experts is no better than (mind, mine, mines).
3. The new grading system has had (quiet, quit, quite) an (affect, effect) on graduate students.

4. Parents will usually (choose, chose) to (advice, advise) (their, there) children at home about religion.
5. Stress is known to (affect, effect) the way (you're, your) performing in the workplace.
6. Last year the members of the band were ready to (quiet, quit, quite), but (know, no, now) they all think (their, there, they're) better than the Dave Matthews band.
7. (Are, Or, Our) accountant is (always, away) from her desk, but (you're, your) welcome to wait.

## Challenge Exercise: Look-Alikes

Circle the word in the parentheses that correctly completes each sentence.

1. Problems with the superego, or what is commonly called a guilty (conscience, conscious), can often (led, lead) to defensive behavior.
2. The life of Dr. Martin Luther King, Jr., was guided by (principals, principles), which (we're, were, where) (taught, thought) to him by his family and church elders.
3. Students who have (pass, passed, past) statewide proficiency tests in reading and mathematics may (loose, lose, loss) sight of other academic goals.
4. Professors often (taught, thought) large lecture classes in the (pass, passed, past), and some still do, but many students (we're, were, where) not able to learn well by that method.
5. The (worse, worst) effects of Darwin's theory of evolution have come from false and (loose, lose, loss, lost) interpretations of his ideas that have been applied to society and economics.
6. The (convenience, convince) of online research has (led, lead) some students to assume that they can do without libraries altogether.
7. The (principal, principle) reason why the nation got (threw, through) the Great Depression of the 1930s was that government leaders not only (taught, thought) about the problems of ordinary people but enacted policies to help them.

# Modifiers

**Modifiers** are descriptive words—**adjectives** and **adverbs**. You use them all the time to make your writing more vivid and specific. They usually will not cause you to make serious grammatical mistakes. However, there are a number of errors that commonly occur with the use of certain adjective and adverb forms.

## Avoiding Double Comparatives

One of these errors to avoid is the **double comparative.** When you compare two things, you use the comparative form of the modifier: one film is *better* than the other; one drink is *sweeter* than another. With longer words, we use the word *more* instead of adding an *–er* ending: one game was *more exciting* than another.

The double comparison is the mistake of using both the *–er* ending and the word *more.*

**Incorrect:**     She is *more smarter* than the other students.

**Correct:**     She is *smarter* than the other students.

In everyday conversation, you may hear combinations like *more better, more happier, more stronger, more bigger, more taller, more faster,* and *more prettier.* Spike Lee used this slang phrasing in the title of his film *Mo' Better Blues.* Such combinations, however, are not standard English. Using these combinations in college writing will create the impression that the writer is uneducated.

---

### TEST YOURSELF: Avoiding Double Comparatives

Identify which of the modifiers in each sentence is incorrect and supply the correct form. In some sentences the modifier may be correct.

1. The book was much longer than I expected.
2. The film we saw last week was more complicated than this one.
3. Jessica has gotten much more thinner since she started the diet.
4. The soccer field is more greener since it has been resurfaced.
5. The music that we listened to in the course was more sophisticated than I expected.
6. The stories we read this term were more simpler than the ones we read last semester.
7. Professor McMurphy gives more higher grades than Professor Jenkins does.

*Answers:* 1. correct 2. correct 3. thinner 4. greener 5. correct 6. simpler 7. higher

---

## Basic Exercise: Avoiding Double Comparatives

Identify which of the modifiers in each sentence is incorrect and supply the correct form. One sentence is correct.

1. Winning the lottery made Josh a more happier man.
2. How much more faster can a train run?
3. The route to the shore is more shorter than you think.
4. Solving this puzzle is more easier than it looks.
5. She had a more better time at the party than her boyfriend.
6. The more later you arrive, the less you will get to eat.
7. The more experienced you are, the better you will do the job.

## Intermediate Exercise: Avoiding Double Comparatives

Identify which of the modifiers in each sentence is incorrect and supply the correct form. One sentence is correct.

1. As goods become more expensive, the demands for more higher wages increase.
2. Tabloids are more easier to read than full-size newspapers but are not more reliable.
3. Jobs that offer more benefits usually require more specialized training.
4. The weather can suddenly turn more cooler in the coastal areas.
5. Americans have become much more heavier in the last decade.
6. Higher scores on statewide tests show that students are becoming more smarter.
7. Some cars have much more better gas mileage than the old gas guzzlers.

## Challenge Exercise: Avoiding Double Comparatives

Identify which of the modifiers in each sentence is incorrect and supply the correct form. There may be more than one error in a sentence. One sentence is correct.

1. Achieving higher income and status levels often makes people feel more greater self-esteem but does not guarantee that they will become more happier.

2. Higher mathematics has its uses not only in the study of science but also in disciplines such as business management and education, where career programs now require more advanced knowledge of mathematics than they once did.

3. The history of the United States can be seen from different perspectives, some of which will yield more deeper insights than others into the experiences of ordinary people.

4. The study of anthropology is more theoretical, but not necessarily more harder, than the study of geography.

5. In some countries the members of the younger generation, because of better nutrition, has become more taller, healthier, and stronger than the generation of their parents.

6. The study of painting, musical composition, and creative writing in colleges has provided more interesting options for students and more fuller appreciation of the arts.

7. Punctuation is a system of marks that has been developed over the centuries to make it much more easier for readers to grasp an author's meaning.

## Avoiding Double Negatives

Another familiar form that you will hear frequently in conversation is the **double negative**—the use of two negative modifiers in the same sentence. In English, unlike some other languages, we use only one negative modifier at a time. In standard English we write, "The copy machine doesn't have any paper left," not "The copy machine doesn't have no paper left." Notice, too, that using a negative with the word *hardly* is also considered a confusing error. Don't write, "She couldn't hardly reach the top shelf." Does that mean that she could just barely reach it or that she couldn't quite reach it? Write either "She could hardly reach the top shelf" or "She couldn't quite reach the top shelf." The words *scarcely* and *barely* also have a negative meaning and should not be used in double negative combinations: "He *could barely* read and write," not "He *couldn't barely* read and write."

In mathematics, a negative times a negative equals a positive. In writing, two negatives can sometimes be used the same way—not to strengthen a negative statement, but to create a positive one. If we say a performer is "not unknown," we mean that she is fairly well known. Or we might say, "The workers won't accept a contract with no raises at all." That means they will demand raises. Except for rare combinations of that kind, however, it's better to avoid doubling your negatives to avoid confusing your readers.

Please note that you may use the combination *neither . . . nor* correctly as a pair of negative words that refer to two separate items. This is not the kind of error that we call a double negative because it doesn't say the same thing twice.

---

### TEST YOURSELF: Avoiding Double Negatives

Decide whether each sentence is correct or contains a double negative. Correct any double negatives.

1. Sam doesn't work here no more.
2. The director has no idea how to improve the performance.
3. The students won't get no diplomas if they don't apply for graduation.
4. Isabel's novel doesn't have a name yet.
5. Careful drivers don't get no credit for following the laws.
6. The parents haven't given the baby a name yet.
7. The store isn't never open on Saturday.

*Answers:* 1. anymore 2. correct 3. any diplomas (or: their diplomas) 4. correct 5. any credit (or: drivers get no credit) 6. correct 7. is never (or: isn't ever)

---

### WRITING EXERCISES: Basic, Intermediate, Challenge

## Basic Exercise: Avoiding Double Negatives

Decide whether each sentence is correct or contains a double negative. Correct any double negatives.

1. If there aren't no more new ideas, we won't solve the problem.
2. Shirley couldn't find no high-paying jobs.
3. It won't make no difference if you don't find the store.
4. Visitors to the site have no idea where to go.
5. These drugs don't have scarcely any side effects.
6. Michael will never have no better friend than James.
7. Charles called the number but nobody didn't answer.

# Intermediate Exercise:
# Avoiding Double Negatives

Decide whether each sentence is correct or contains a double negative. Correct any double negatives.

1. Increased profits for large companies don't necessarily create no new jobs in big cities.
2. Some urban legends are true, but others don't have no basis in fact.
3. The ordinary citizen can't hardly tell whether the news media are providing all the facts about important events.
4. Since the restaurant raised its prices, not as many customers go there no more.
5. A person who doesn't have a college education usually can't find an interesting, well-paying job.
6. It doesn't take no genius to guess how the plot of the film will end.
7. Not being able to find no parking places prevents many people from driving into the city from the suburbs.

# Challenge Exercise:
# Avoiding Double Negatives

Decide whether each sentence is correct or contains a double negative. Correct any double negatives.

1. Opponents of the death penalty argue that no other industrialized countries, especially those in western Europe, don't practice capital punishment.
2. The Baby Boomers, or the generation born after World War II that came of age in the 1960s, didn't have none of the same values as their parents' generation.
3. A poem with no figures of speech, such as similes and metaphors, will probably have neither emotional power nor stylistic intensity.
4. Studying archaeology using DNA analysis is revealing facts about the prehistoric world that no scientists never even guessed before.
5. During the Renaissance and for several centuries afterward most educated people did not see no aesthetic value in the great Gothic cathedrals of thirteenth-century France.
6. No developing countries that fail to develop successful trade policies can hardly ever achieve strong economic growth.

7. Because of the extensive exploration of Mars by unmanned vehicles, many scientists believe it isn't necessary to plan no human flights to the red planet in the near future.

## Some Problems with Adverbs

You probably know the difference between adjectives and adverbs (see the section on Parts of Speech, p. 139), and you probably get them right most of the time. The **adverbs** are mostly adjectives with –ly endings added: He threw *quickly* with *quick* hands. You should also distinguish between *slow* as an adjective (a *slow* journey) and *slowly* as an adverb (we traveled *slowly*).

Certain adverbs, however, are often written in the wrong form. The most common example is *good* used incorrectly as an adverb instead of *well*. It is not correct standard English to write "She did *good*"—not, at least, unless you mean that she performed acts of charity. If you mean she performed effectively, you should write "She did *well*."

A similar nonstandard form is the word *real* in place of *really*. You will often hear people (especially less educated people) say, "That was *real* interesting," or "I know her *real* well." These statements should be "That was *really* interesting" or "I know her *really* well." The adjective *easy* already ends in y, so you may find yourself trying to use it as an adverb instead of the correct form, *easily*. Notice the difference between "She chose an *easy* route" and "She completed the route *easily*." *Easy* tells *what kind* of, and therefore is an adjective; *easily* tells *how*, and is therefore an adverb.

---

### TEST YOURSELF: Problems with Adverbs

Correct any mistakes in the use of adverbs.

1. The band's live performances are real exciting.
2. Turn the corner quick and drive up the ramp.
3. Allison made a really beautiful collage of her friends' pictures.
4. This truck doesn't run so good in cold weather.
5. Remember this cell phone number well; you may need it.
6. Leon sang the passage a little too slow for my taste.
7. The facial details made the picture look real authentic.

*Answers:* 1. really 2. quickly 3. correct 4. run so well 5. correct 6. slowly 7. really

---

## Basic Exercise: Problems with Adverbs

Find and correct any errors in the use of *quick/quickly, slow/slowly, good/well, real/really,* and *easy/easily.* One sentence is correct.

1. The contestant was real smart and well informed.
2. Do the assignment quick so that we can leave on time.
3. She did a real good job with the project.
4. This car runs good and has good gas mileage.
5. It is an easy dance to learn.
6. We were surprised at how quick Carlos learned the lesson.
7. She sang real well last night.

## Intermediate Exercise: Problems with Adverbs

Find and correct any errors in the use of *quick/quickly, slow/slowly, good/well, real/really,* and *easy/easily.* One sentence is correct.

1. Few smokers can give up the habit very easy even though they know smoking is harming their health.
2. Customers can find discounts on camcorders and digital cameras very quick on the Internet.
3. A real vigorous workout at a gym leaves you feeling totally relaxed.
4. Financial advisers generally tell people not to expect sudden wealth but to acquire financial independence slow over a number of years.
5. The state government is not likely to find a quick and easy solution to such a complicated problem.
6. Students who don't type very good should use one of the online typing courses to improve their speed and accuracy.
7. The representatives of the student government made a real intelligent decision when they voted to create a weekly student newspaper.

## Challenge Exercise: Problems with Adverbs

Find and correct any errors in the use of *quick/quickly, slow/slowly, good/well, real/really,* and *easy/easily.* One sentence is correct.

1. Changes in society's perception of gender roles do not happen quick, but even small changes make a big difference in the way people live.
2. Film critics are sometimes slow to recognize outstanding films which introduce cinematic styles that depart from Hollywood conventions.
3. The term *paradigm shift* is commonly used to denote a transformation of intellectual structures that causes a real dramatic change in society, government, education, or technology.
4. Graduate programs in education now require students not only to study the theory and practice of pedagogy but also to learn at least one academic discipline real well.
5. Although one party or the other has won easy in some congressional and presidential elections, there have also been many closely fought races in which the winner was not known until a thorough count was completed.
6. Students with serious learning disabilities may not be able to learn to read, write, or do mathematical calculations as quick as the typical learner, but that does not mean that they cannot learn just as much.
7. Statistical studies in education and medicine cannot produce results as precise as those of controlled scientific experiments because students and medical patients cannot be isolated easy like mice in a laboratory.

# Articles in ESL Writing

The little words *the*, *a*, and *an* (they are called **articles**) seldom cause problems for native speakers, who learn to use them correctly, or nearly correctly, as small children. Most native speakers never learned rules about using articles; they just use them by habit. If English is not your first language, however, and if you learned English in the classroom rather than by speaking it frequently with native speakers, you may find it difficult to know when to use these little words. Some languages have similar articles; some do not. Even those that do have them often use them in slightly different ways. Therefore they tend to cause problems for writers who use English as a second language.

Do not be discouraged if you continue to make small errors in the use of articles and if you have difficulty understanding the rules for using them. There are many exceptions, and the important thing is to develop correct habits by listening to spoken English frequently. However, it may help you to remember some basic patterns.

*A* and *an* are called **indefinite articles** because they are used before nouns that do not have definite, specific identities. For example, *a* school, *an* office, *a* proposal, *an* opinion—in using these phrases the author is not referring to a specific school, office, proposal, or opinion. If she writes *the* school, *the* office, *the* proposal, or *the* opinion, she has a specific school, office, proposal, or opinion in mind. The articles *a* and *an* are used to make general statements. We might say, "She went to *a* supermarket," meaning that we don't know what particular store it was. "I was watching *a* parade" means that I choose not to identify the particular parade. The difference between *a* and *an* is based on the sound of following word. Words that begin with vowel sounds take *an*: *an* apple, *an* opinion, *an* open door. The article *a* is used for all words beginning with consonant sounds: *a* bodega, *a* space shuttle, *a* billion dollars.

What mistakes do second-language writers often make? Probably the most common is to leave out articles that should be included in a sentence. This happens most with students whose first languages do not use articles. They might write, "People come to United States to get better jobs." Why must we say *the* United States? Why do we read *the* newspaper or *a* newspaper, but we don't just "read newspaper"?

Perhaps one source of confusion is that we usually leave out articles with plural forms: It is correct to say we "read newspapers." We usually say, "I went to *the* supermarket" or "I saw *the* parade." But in plural statements we might say, "I like to shop in *supermarkets*" or "I enjoy watching *parades*." Notice the difference.

Another mistake is to put articles where they don't belong. We usually do not use articles before specific names of persons, products, cities, and colleges, and the like unless the word *the* is already part of the name. Write "She worked at General Motors," not "She worked at *the* General Motors" or "He liked to play chess," not "He liked to play *the* chess."

---

**TEST YOURSELF: Using *a, an,* and *the***

Look for missing articles, incorrect articles, or articles that should be deleted. One sentence is correct.

1. Alfredo decided to buy new netbook.
2. The first question on test is tricky.

3. Tenesha isn't sure she has opinion on the subject.
4. Sharon enjoys playing the Scrabble.
5. Ronald looked for a parking spot near the stadium.
6. Paul thought that eating a apple would help him feel better.
7. The stranger knocked loudly on door with his fist.

*Answers:* 1. a new netbook 2. on the test 3. an opinion 4. playing Scrabble 5. correct
6. an apple 7. the door

---

WRITING EXERCISES: Basic, Intermediate, Challenge

# Basic Exercise: Using *a, an,* and *the*

Look for the missing article, incorrect article, or article that should be deleted in each sentence. One sentence is correct.

1. Kit looked for new suit to wear to the interview.
2. The last paragraph of your essay is not on topic.
3. Theodore doesn't have address yet.
4. Karen is hoping to attend the Yale University.
5. The sound of Lester's saxophone could be heard from the street.
6. The children were excited about seeing a ostrich in the zoo.
7. The previews were so exciting they made film seem boring.

# Intermediate Exercise: Using *a, an,* and *the*

Look for missing articles, incorrect articles, or articles that should be deleted. There may be more than one error in a sentence. One sentence is correct.

1. Credit card debt has become major problem in the United States.
2. Hispanic Americans are becoming largest minority group in the country.
3. The athletes who compete in Olympics are tested frequently for banned substances.
4. Religious institutions disagree on subject of gay marriage.
5. For a appeal to be successful, the defense attorney has to find technical flaw in the proceedings.
6. Some vacation spots remain popular despite fact that they are overcrowded.
7. A best-selling novel will not always make a exciting film if the director cannot capture tone and style of the author.

## Challenge Exercise: Using *a*, *an*, and *the*

Look for missing articles, incorrect articles, or articles that should be deleted. There may be more than one error in each sentence. One sentence is correct.

1. Shakespeare's history plays teach lessons about leadership and responsibility in age of political intrigue.
2. Exercise physiology is a academic discipline that offers knowledge and training for students who hope to become physical therapists, physical education instructors, and gymnastics coaches.
3. Some mathematical theorems have taken centuries to prove, one of most famous being Fermat's theorem.
4. The proliferation of Web sites on all academic subjects has made process of writing research papers more complicated than in past.
5. Although objective tests serve some indispensable functions, many experts question the way they are being used to serve a whole range of purposes without adequate verification.
6. The development of market economies in most of countries of central and eastern Europe has been uneven and difficult but not without some successes.
7. The purpose of a ethnographic study is to understand the inner experience of group by close and extended observation of a few examples.

# Word Choice

Learn to choose the best words to convey your meaning. **Diction**, which means word choice, is an essential aspect of effective writing. Words should be accurate, precise, and specific. That is, they should mean exactly what you want them to say. You know how annoying it is if someone gives you the wrong directions to find an address or incorrect instructions on how to do something. It can also be annoying when someone is not specific enough. A friend wants to introduce you to a potential boyfriend, and you want to know more about him. "He's a nice person," your friend says—and that tells you just about zero of what you really want to know. *Nice*, one of those catchall words like *good*, *great*, and *interesting*, is not usually the most specific word available. Be careful as well with words like *all*, *everybody*, *nobody*, *most*, *many*, *some*, and *a few*. In conversation we make casual remarks like "Everybody knows that song." Whoever is listening understands that *everybody* doesn't mean every single person in the world. In college writing on serious subjects, however, you should make more exact statements. "Everybody wants stricter enforcement of drug laws" is not a precise statement. *Most people* would probably be a safe phrase in this statement; *many people* or *some people* would be too weak.

As you learn new vocabulary, do not be afraid to use it in your writing. Just be sure to check the meaning in a dictionary first. When you begin noticing a particular new word in your reading, you may guess at the meaning—and guess wrong. "This will *exacerbate* the condition"; "This will *alleviate* the condition." Which word do you want? What is a *retroactive* policy? What does it mean to *defer* payment? What exactly do we refer to as a *story*, a *novel*, a *poem*, or a work of *prose*? If you hope to be a careful writer, you should always use your dictionary when choosing words.

## Some Often Misused Words

Study this list of words to see whether you understand all of them and know how to use them in your sentences.

1. **accept** Remember that you *accept* an invitation, but the host invites everyone **except** people he doesn't like.
2. **aggravate** This word means "to make something worse." Many people use it in conversation interchangeably with **irritate**, which means "to annoy." Note the difference: "Your gum chewing irritates me" and "Your gum chewing will *aggravate* your toothache."
3. **allusion** To make an *allusion* when you write, or to *allude* to something, means to refer to it a bit indirectly. Don't confuse this word with **illusion**, which means a false idea about something.
4. **amount** Use this word to refer to a total or mass of something such as liquid, money, or sugar. Use the word **number** for items that can be counted: a large *number* of people, packages, or questions.
5. **anxious** *Anxious* means "full of anxiety," "tense," or "nervous." If you mean to say that someone really wants to do something, use eager: "I am eager (not *anxious*) to join the project."
6. **biweekly/bimonthly** *Biweekly* normally means "every two weeks"; bimonthly means "every two months." But people often

use these terms when they mean **semiweekly** or **semimonthly**, or twice weekly or twice monthly. If you want to be sure that no one misunderstands you, you'd better write *every two weeks* or *twice a week* to prevent any mistakes.

7. **disinterested** Although people often use this word loosely to mean the same thing as **uninterested,** which means "lacking interest" or "bored," *disinterested* has a more important useful meaning. A *disinterested* party in a negotiation is one who has nothing to gain; the word means "unbiased" and "not having any personal stake in a matter."

8. **empathy** *Empathy* means imagining that you experience exactly what another person experiences but without necessarily feeling sorry for the other person. We send **sympathy** cards, but not *empathy* cards. You *empathize* with someone by imagining yourself in that person's situation; you *sympathize* with someone by feeling sorry for him or her.

9. **enormity** Don't confuse this word with **enormous.** *Enormity* usually refers to an outrageous, monstrous event. To avoid confusion, if you want to stress the sheer size of something, use words like *vastness, hugeness,* or *magnitude* that do not also contain the idea of evil.

10. **ingenuous** This word looks like **ingenious**, but it doesn't mean smart. *Ingenuous* means "simple or naïve": "He is ingenuous enough to be taken in by that scheme."

11. **liable** *Liable* means to be responsible for something, in the legal sense of having to pay if something goes wrong, as in "You'll be *liable* for the whole amount if you don't pay on time." It can be used to suggest that something undesirable may happen, as in "Sam is *liable* to be sorry he quit his job." It's better to use **likely** for something good that may happen, as in "Sam is *likely* to be promoted."

12. **minority** Mathematically, a *minority* is simply a quantity less than half, and a **majority** is more than half. Because ethnic groups that make up less than half of the population have been called *minority groups,* some people identify particular groups with the term *minorities.* However, most people don't like the label *minority,* maybe because the word *minor* that it contains seems to indicate something unimportant.

13. **quote** To *quote* someone is to repeat exactly the words he or she used, which means putting the words in quotation marks

when you are writing. However, remember that you are *quoting* the author, and the author *writes* or *argues*. Do not write that the author *quotes*.

14. **respectively** This word, unlike **respectfully**, has nothing to do with respect. It means "in the order provided." For example, you might write, "Paula and Jeremy were elected president and vice president, *respectively*."

15. **unique** This word really means "one of a kind." Unfortunately, too often people use it to describe something that is merely unusual or special. Try to respect its meaning and use it only to describe someone or something that stands alone.

---

### TEST YOURSELF: Misused Words

Determine whether the italicized word in each sentence is used correctly. If it is not, substitute a better word or change the phrasing of the sentence to make it correct.

1. Since Carmen earns $500 a week, she makes $1000 *bimonthly*.
2. A large *amount* of people attended the workshop.
3. Your cell phone going off every two minutes really *aggravates* me.
4. That long introduction left me totally *disinterested*.
5. Shatisha spoke very *respectively* to her father, but he wouldn't listen.
6. Pete was so *ingenuous* he was able to solve my computer problem.
7. I like the way the novel *quotes* at the beginning, "It was the best of times."

*Answers:* 1. biweekly or twice a month 2. number of people 3. annoys me 4. uninterested or bored 5. respectfully 6. ingenious 7. the novel begins,

---

### WRITING EXERCISES: Basic, Intermediate, Challenge

## Basic Exercise: Misused Words

Determine whether the italicized word in each sentence is used correctly. If it is not, substitute a better word or change the phrasing of the sentence to make it correct.

1. All of the films I saw this year were truly *unique*.
2. EZ-Pass allows much larger *amounts* of cars to pass through toll booths every hour.
3. Jeremy thinks he is *liable* to win the student government election.
4. Larry is really *anxious* to earn his pilot's license.

5. The girl in the story *quotes,* "I finally made it."
6. All of the students *except* Maggie took the test.
7. I don't have any *allusions* about winning the competition.

## Intermediate Exercise: Misused Words

Determine whether the italicized word in each sentence is used correctly. If it is not, substitute a better word or change the phrasing of the sentence to make it correct.

1. The high pollen count yesterday *aggravated* allergic reactions throughout the county.
2. Courses in Excel and Access are given in March and April, *respectively.*
3. The candidate for mayor was elected by a very large *minority.*
4. The *enormity* of the crowds required the planners to move the event to another site.
5. The family members sent a card to their neighbor expressing *empathy* for the loss of her mother.
6. The public may find it difficult to *except* the mayor's changes in the school system.
7. The *amount* of e-mail messages and letters provoked by the candidate's remarks was startling.

## Challenge Exercise: Misused Words

Compose sentences of your own using the following words correctly.

1. allusion
2. disinterested
3. respectively
4. ingenuous
5. minority
6. enormity
7. aggravate

## Key Words from Chapter 12 for Review

adjectives, adverbs, articles, common nouns, diction, double comparative, double negative, indefinite articles, look-alikes, modifiers, proper nouns

# QUICK REFERENCE GUIDE TO TOPICS OF GRAMMAR

# credits

Linda Acredolo, Ph.D., and Susan Goodwyn, Ph.D. Excerpt from *Baby Signs: How to Talk with Your Baby Before Your Baby Can Talk* (New York: McGraw-Hill, Contemporary Books, 2002), pp. 43–44.

*Baseball Almanac.* 2005 American League Team Standings from *Baseball Almanac*, http://www.baseball-almanac.com/yearly/yr2005a.shtml. Reprinted by permission of *Baseball Almanac*.

David Berlinski. Excerpt from *A Tour of the Calculus* (New York: Vintage, 1995), p. 308.

Jorge Luis Borges. "Dreamtigers," from *Collected Fictions* by Jorge Luis Borges, translated by Andrew Hurley, copyright © 1998 by Maria Kodama; translation copyright © 1998 by Penguin Putnam Inc. Used by permission of Viking Penguin, a division of Penguin Group (USA) Inc. and Penguin Group (Canada), a Division of Pearson Canada Inc.

Marshall Brian and Jeff Tyson. Information from "How Cell Phones Work," from *How Stuff Works.* January 17, 2004. http://www.electronics.howstuffworks.com/cellphone.htm

Jared Diamond. Excerpt from "How China Became Chinese," *Guns, Germs, and Steel: The Fates of Human Societies* (New York: Norton, 1997), p. 323.

Jin Ha. Excerpt from *The Crazed* (New York: Vintage, 2002). P. 304.

Judith Harris. Excerpt from *The Nurture Assumption: Why Children Turn Out the Way They Do* (New York: The Free Press, 1998), pp. 169–170.

Howard Jones. Excerpt from *Mutiny on the Amistad* (New York: Oxford University Press, 1987), p. 8.

Jamaica Kincaid. "Girl" from *At the Bottom of the River* by Jamaica Kincaid. Copyright © 1983 by Jamaica Kincaid. Reprinted by permission of Farrar, Straus and Giroux, LLC.

Jhumpa Lahiri. Excerpt from *Interpreter of Maladies* (New York: Houghton Mifflin, 1999), p. 114.

Chang-Rae Lee. Excerpt from *Native Speaker* (New York: Riverhead Books, 1995), p. 65.

Gabriel José García Márquez. Information from *Living to Tell the Tale*, trans. Edith Grossman (New York: Knopf, 2003).

Steven Pinker. Excerpt from *The Blank Slate* (New York: Viking, 2002), p. 197.

*Professional Guide to Diseases*, 5th ed. (Springhouse, PA: Springhouse Corporation, 1995), pp. 409–411.

Brent Staples. Excerpt from *Parallel Time: Growing Up in Black and White* (New York: Avon Books, 1994), p. 36.

Amy Tan. Information from "Amy Tan: Best-Selling Novelist," *Academy of Achievement.* January 17, 2004. http://www.achievement.org/autodoc/page/tan0bio-1

U.S. Census Bureau. Table: Median Income of Households by Selected Characteristics, 2004; U.S. Census Bureau, *Income, Poverty, and Health Insurance Coverage in the United States: 2004.* Web source: http://www.census.gov Found at Infoplease.com (Pearson Education).

Michael Zweig. Excerpt from *The Working Class Majority: America's Best Kept Secret* (Ithaca and London: Cornell University Press, 2000), p. 11.

# index of critical terms

INDEX OF CRITICAL TERMS